To Paul,

With gratitude

and good wishes

Beverley Laska

THE PROPHECIES FOR CHURCH AND STATE

the PROPHECIES *for* CHURCH & STATE

Beverley Tasker

Loebertas, Long Ashton, England

First published in 1992
by Loebertas
7 Church Lane, Long Ashton, Bristol BS18 9LU

ISBN 1 874316 01 5
(Paperback)
ISBN 1 874316 00 7
(Hardback)

Typeset in Goudy by KJ Studios Limited, Bristol
Printed by Dotesios Limited, Trowbridge, Wilts.

Preface

Many accept that the world is facing a crisis. Not everyone agrees about the nature of this crisis, nor is a solution readily to hand. It seems, however, that the character of the twentieth century - with its divisions, factions and trends - has been deeply influenced by secularism and a widespread rejection of God. Tragically, the world's religions have added to the present plight in their preoccupation with finance and the complexities of self-survival. They no longer speak to the soul.

Time is running out. If the human race persists in following the course it has adopted, catastrophe cannot be far off. Radical action is necessary. We must repudiate those voices that say all is well, and urgently try to recognise where we have gone wrong. Only then can foundations be laid for a truly spiritual, intellectual and ethical recovery.

The Prophecies for Church and State were recorded over a period of twenty years. They will not be well received in every quarter, but they are offered as a contribution to the enormous task ahead.

H.B.T
October 1992

Contents

THE PROLOGUE

THE CALL

LETTERS TO A FRACTURED SOCIETY

THE DISCOURSE   265

THE EPILOGUE

INDEX

THE
PROLOGUE

— I —

SPIRIT OF DESOLATION

Midway in the Journey

What do the days mean to me
as they pass by without hope?

What of the hours of study
and the patient toil with words?

Where is the integrity which once I knew,
the confidence of days in the bloom of youth?

Ideals shattered as broken glass,
upon them my heart has bled.

Friends, companions and laughter,
all gone as ghosts in the night.

I am alone in the world of dread,
afraid to stand, to think ashamed.

The Secrets of God

I do not understand the world,
nor can I see the mysteries of God.

The purpose of life eludes me;
the facts of existence are a cause of despair.

Why do men fret and argue together
and lose themselves in strife?

Why does the sweetness of life turn sour
and the blossom become but dust?

Surely there is an answer but it is not in me.
The secrets of God I cannot find.

Why does my mouth rule my soul
and my spirit bow down to my tongue?

Why do I speak of things of remorse
and torture my soul with doubt?

Why do I hurt those I love
and confuse their innocent hearts?

Surely there is an answer but it is not in me.
The secrets of God I cannot find.

Ashes to Ashes

I am caught in the vacuum of nothingness,
    there is not a pure thought in my mind.

The world is grey and without joy;
    vision is darkened by the state of my soul.

There is no pleasure in simple things;
    the complexion of life reflects my existence:

it is a sphere of decreasing circumference,
    spiralling towards the centre,

hurtling to self destruction,
    plunging into desolation.

As fields that surround our cities
    are waste covering blackened grass,

so is the soul confronted by its finitude,
    wretched in the grip of mortality,

made worse by the love of friends,
    confounded by memories of the past.

It is a truly miserable state of affairs
    to be faced with the collapse of being.

Cursed are the limitations of the human will,
    impotent to act in a universe of decay.

Loss of Trust

I feel the awe of the infinite
but with people I am lost.

The heights and depths of experience
are crushed to nothing by humankind.

Failures are stronger than success,
for note is taken of our mistakes.

There is no comfort in Christian charity;
goodwill receives no mercy from the world.

If one builds on the esteem of men
one lives from hour to hour;

if one looks for praise in doing well
the world gives little in return.

Nothing is so fickle as the human mind;
from moment to moment its affections change.

If you base your life on the opinions of men
it will crash like a house in ruins.

Do not look to man for your strength –
the world will leave you desolate.

The church, politics and your neighbour
are part of the desolation.

— II —

ANCIENT
AND MODERN

The Prophet's Birth

I was born in the midst of the horrors of war,
    in grey days of monuments and ruins,

when men, women and their children
    were slaughtered and butchered by design.

Efficient causes led to extermination
    by gas chambers, firing squads and ovens:

Auschwitz, Dachau and the Nazi regime,
    unequalled in human history.

Innocent lives, once cherished and loved,
    were selected, tortured and destroyed,

while safe men closed their eyes
    saying shh! it is not happening –

man is not capable of such things,
    of torture and of calculated death.

Statistics smoothed over by subsequent generations –
    let us forget and remember no more!

Why remind ourselves of war?
    Let us enjoy the present and ignore the past!

So the lessons are not grafted in our hearts;
    we begin to drift in the same direction.

Seeds of Decay

How easy it has been for the cynic
to prepare the way for our decline!

Anything of nobility and honour,
of beauty and delicate form,

built over hundreds of years,
created by sensitive minds,

now victim of pragmatic judgement,
condemned by an aimless generation.

How wisdom, afraid, defers to youth!
How brash youth despises the past!

The dimension of time disappears
by devotion to the present.

Truly the penalty will be paid
by our children's children;

they will curse this generation
and burn the images of our time.

The Contemporary Scene

Is there peace and quiet in the land?
　Let it be mocked by the modern mind!

Is there a place of solitude and silence?
　Let the noisy generation condemn!

Is there a little worship in our lives?
　Let modern man be full of laughter!

Is there a little wisdom among us?
　Let the people reel and scorn!

Is there a voice for decency and respect?
　Let those without stand and jeer!

Is there any beauty in the world?
　Let the unquiet soul shout for change!

These are the words of contemporary man –
　all is old fashioned and out of date.

But this resentment of ancient things
　has already passed into tradition.

A Liberal Society

Consider the abuses of freedom,
how easily they can destroy!

How liberty becomes a cloak
to cover evil intentions and desires!

Protagonists of free expression
restrict others by their protests.

Speech descends into inarticulation
and debate is subject to the loudest voice.

Intellectuals deceive the innocent
and lead them into the ways of death.

Individuals create enormous wealth
by theft, extortion and vice.

Men hide behind their rules and conventions,
afraid to have the truth declared.

The evils of men are smoothed over
by those who fear the truth to be known.

Doctrines of Man

How bad manners become the rule
   as parents withdraw their authority!

How the sense of judgement is impaired
   by excusing every kind of behaviour!

Sport has lost its skill and pride
   and is a tool for commercial gain.

Humour is sick, repetitive and crude,
   and comedians sink into depravation.

Practitioners of free art and theatre
   turn their liberties to crime and sin.

Literature has been degraded
   and is replaced by a visual screen.

Literacy stands for elitism
   and is ridiculed at home and school.

Children are corrupted by political dogma
   and taught to be hard in a hardening world.

Harvest of Ruin

I see the results of our secular ways
  and the consequence of our evil deeds.

There is dereliction in our cities
  and hypocrisy in all our schemes.

The state asserts its superiority
  as the freedom of man declines.

The law traps the innocent
  while the cunning have their way.

Governments develop social aid
  but the fibre of life is destroyed.

Church and state combine in indolence
  to put the gifts of the Spirit aside.

Progress obliterates the past
  and leaves ruin in its wake.

All this unrecognised by our leaders,
  who are arrogant and ignorant of our malaise.

— III —

CITY OF CENOTAPHS

Lost Inheritance

I lived in the city,
  in a terraced house on the hill,

and I saw the great demolition
  of perfectly respectable homes:

millions of people displaced as in war,
  houses torn down, their heritage despised;

misery caused by council votes,
  and a smell of corruption in the air;

markets and stalls sent to the wall,
  characters banished from towns;

beautiful arcades and coffee houses
  lost for ever in the planner's dream,

replaced by vast concrete towers –
  cities ravished by imperious schemes.

The Spiral

Where is the character of urban life?
It is buried beneath the concrete blocks.

Consider the ancient city –
broad spread of industrial decay.

Consider the modern city –
conglomeration of architectural clay.

See those miles of accommodation
where humans are housed in their warrens:

motorways strangle their freedom
in a huge, grey, dull world.

Where is the character of urban life?
It is buried beneath the concrete blocks!

O this nation of genius and respected past,
creating a future of horror and gloom –

a claustrophobic land of ugly cities
which eventually will suffocate us all!

Urban Sickness

Which comes first in our cities –
a slum dwelling or a slum mind?

Give some a beautiful home,
    it will be ruined in a year;

remove others to hard conditions,
    their lives will be deranged.

Large families in crowded conditions
    await bureaucratic decisions;

good property decays around them
    as corporations hold debates.

Why should families in towns
    be subject to political ineptitude?

Year after year of delay
    the generations wait.

Which comes first in our cities –
    a slum dwelling or a slum mind?

False Priorities

Here is the cause of our discontents:
  a wealthy land with the wrong priorities –

heavily taxed and misdirected
  our gains are thrown away.

Speculative programmes at great expense
  do not provide the destitute with food.

A person is valued less than property
  and offices are more important than homes.

A complex life sets the pattern of inequality;
  a confused nation multiplies its faults.

Lament

O this tragic generation, why have we deserted God?
Why are we so hard and brittle in our ways?

Why have we allowed our freedom to be bound,
    building cities where man cannot thrive?

Why sacrifice love and human respect
    to the creations of our hands?

It is too late to turn again
    from the machinations of our minds.

The Plans of Men

Men will invent their schemes
and voice their plans for the future,

but they will come to nothing,
they will vanish like a puff of smoke.

Men continue to ignore the Lord their God,
therefore their dreams will turn to dust:

all their hopes for urban development
will remain on the shelves of city halls;

all their aims for human achievement
will be sterile in their troubled minds.

Because they doubt the Christian faith
the standard of life will fall;

because they have no heart for God
their thoughts will come to an end.

— IV —

GRAVEN IMAGES

A Desirable Residence

I lived on the latest estate –
cardboard houses for the material man,

each competing through his possessions,
his wife, his children, his work;

each seeking to outclass his neighbour –
where have you been? what have you done? –

each man doing the right thing
as prescribed and approved by his class,

with sufficient interest in voluntary work
to sustain one's place in the community.

Golf on Thursday, squash on Friday,
sailing on Saturday, motoring on Sunday;

lawn in the evening after the papers,
correct conversation and the right kind of sherry.

People coming round for supper,
correct and making their mark.

By the way, how is the children's education?
Oh, we're sending them away to school.

Is that painting an original or merely a print?
It hangs very nicely in the corner of the room.

Oh, what a beautiful lampshade you have!
 (And damn you it's nicer than ours!)

Goodnight, and thank you for a lovely time!
 It's a pleasure old boy – see you again and again

till we grow sick and tired without hope
 and seek a move to the south, or the north, or abroad,

taking our culture with us
 and our memories to compare.

Keep trying, you qualified nomads.
 Eventually you will settle – in the dust!

The Financial Capital

Come to London,
   where the weakest go to the wall,

a beautiful city plunging into chaos,
   its history raped by developers;

a city in the hands of powerful men
   whose methods stop at nothing –

frenzied men in the Strand
   who calculate their profits by the hour,

who substitute a love of mammon
   for the living word of God.

As petals fall across St. James' Park
   and the pale sun glints through dead branches,

come, see its life before it disappears,
   before the walls become its tomb,

new buildings replacing old,
   before the memory fades.

The Ill-To-Do

Observe the corruption of the rich –
   idle speculators in land and wealth,

who use money to buy their freedom
   and gather luxuries in their arms;

who are empty with unlawful possessions
   and gross with an abundance of goods;

who abuse the gentle nature of the people
   and rob the innocent of their dues;

who bring about disintegration
   and imbalance to the structures of power.

These are the ones at the root of our trouble:
   greedy men who have lost their God,

who plunge the nation into confusion
   because they despise God's laws.

It is no solution to tax their wealth.
   Great things come only from a change of heart.

Gross National Product

The crisis has come upon us;
we have ignored warnings of old.

My people have lost their souls
in their chase after false gods.

Man strives to better his neighbour
collecting a warehouse of goods;

rather he strove to better his soul
and put possessions in their rightful place.

How far do we go before we learn?
How much longer can we pretend?

What will happen when confusion comes
from the collapse of inflated ideas?

Who will lead us when the crash occurs
and our all-embracing theories fail?

Credit to All

We are a nation in debt,
  living beyond our means,

buying goods we cannot afford,
  spending more than we receive:

expensive clothing on account,
  large cars on increasing loans;

mortgaged from birth to death,
  owning things that are not ours;

possessing houses we do not own,
  owing debts we cannot pay;

paying with money that belongs to others,
  settling accounts after long delays.

All this is wrong!
  It is not the way of peace –

this way of life that consumes our character,
  this way of life that inflates our greed.

The Cost of Living

Cursed by the desire to spend
we have falsified existence.

Like a balloon that is over inflated
the nation will expand till it bursts.

We have created the problems for ourselves
and waste time trying to solve them,

pretending we are busy when we are not,
afraid to admit that we only pretend.

We heave and strain to support our lives
and lose ourselves in strife.

Obsessed with employment and productivity
we have forgotten the purpose of human life.

Why do we need our annual increments
but to spend on goods which pass away?

Incredibly we all pursue the wind
and boast as it eludes us.

The Crash!

The hurricane of wrath has struck,
wrecking our plans and possessions.

The whirlwind of greed is upon us,
spiralling down to desolation.

Like a tree trunk that is rotting,
so is a nation of greedy men:

its collapse brings down the branches
and the whole decays into dust.

— v —

THE POOR

Blessed are the Poor

I saw the poor of the earth
in their endeavour to survive,

and my heart was filled with sorrow
to witness man's injustice to man.

I heard the anguish of those in need
and the cries of their despair.

I felt the bitterness of their complaint
and brought the matter to the Lord,

but no answer came –
instead a silence and a watchful eye.

The Destitute

Consider the poor of the world;
  suffer the injustice of their lot.

Do not sweep them aside,
  we are judged by their plight:

their sorrow and pain is ours,
  their sadness and empty eyes.

As a man sees his wife and children starve
  the rich man calculates his wealth.

As little children lose their hope
  the west indulges in greed.

As parents fear for the future
  the west lusts after goods.

As we argue for increased wages
  a million children starve to death.

As we spend our gains on cigarettes and beer
  a million parents die in despair.

Who is concerned for the poor,
  the hungry and those without homes?

A nation that ceases to care about others
  is a nation near the end.

The Underprivileged

Consider those who live in decaying conditions
declared unfit for human habitation,

who are humiliated beyond endurance
and suffer at the hands of the state.

Bless them for bearing our sins
and for shielding us from our faults.

A society that has no compassion
has put them where they are.

We treat the helpless with derision
and pretend that we help the poor;

we treat them as second class citizens
and prevent them from improving their lives.

We prefer to spend our money on leisure
and fail to ensure human life is secure;

we hope to live in a dream world
but their problems we choose to ignore.

Concerning Equality

The world is divided between rich and poor.
Man, therefore, is not at peace.

The rich man chooses what to eat;
    the poor man cannot choose to eat.

The rich man despises the poor
    because the poor disturb his conscience.

The rich man buys goods with his money
    but the poor man buys money with his goods.

The rich man goes here and there
    but the poor remain where they are.

The rich man multiplies his goods
    but the poor diminish in return.

The rich man blames the poor for their plight
    but the poor are poor because others are rich.

The rich man is judged by his wealth:
    let the sentence be passed –

less for the rich
    and more for the poor!

— VI —

THEMES
OF INDUSTRY

Journey Through the Cities

I journeyed through the cities
and there I saw a loss of hope:

men and women unemployed,
anxious to do a day's work –

victims of the machine of industry,
waste material of an economic world –

struggling to keep their pride
as society passed them by;

walking forsaken streets
in search of forgotten signs;

fighting to maintain their families,
to give their children cause for joy;

depressed by the circumstance of change,
or by the policies of the age.

What glory here in the modern world?
What reward from the march of time?

The Industrial Legacy

The industrial revolution has bred discontent,
the machine has brought unease.

Great movements of work in the land
have achieved little for the being of man.

Forces of labour in the nation
have not brought happiness to humankind.

Mass production, schemes and unions
have combined to bring us to ruin.

Blocks of power have been created
which tread down the man in the street.

Workers follow their leaders
like sheep to the slaughter.

The Virtues of Change

Have monopolies kept prices down?
Or trade unions improved the human lot?

Has nationalisation helped the working man?
Or social science brought poverty to an end?

Have combined resources increased employment?
Has mass production reduced queues for the dole?

Have railways improved after rationalisation?
Has nationalised coal made a cheaper fire?

Have mergers brought lasting success?
Has legislation allowed freedom to grow?

Has the morale of the nation increased
as we start again, cut back, and fail?

There is a gap between ideas and practice,
a gulf between the mind and the hand.

Unemployment Figures

Consider the thousands of elderly people
who could be visited by men out of work.

Consider the hospital services,
destitute of labour while men are unemployed.

Consider the decaying city centres
while we say there is no work to be done.

Consider the rubbish lying in towns
as men stand in line for the dole.

Consider all the possible sources of employment
as we pretend to find a solution.

Consider the vast areas of human potential
as men waste away on social aid.

No man can be proud to serve on the dole;
no country can afford payment for no work.

There is no will in government or people;
we make excuses as the land decays.

Elegy for Industry

O this land of discontent,
  unable to mend her ways!

Like a casting overheated
  and cracked in its mould,

molten and pouring everywhere
  with sparks and cries of alarm,

this land is broken,
  the mould is to be thrown away.

— VII —

THE AUTHORITY OF STATE

In Re Publica

I see the cost of progress
  in a world removed from its past,

the erosion of personal liberty
  for the sake of efficiency and method.

I see the subjugation of the person
  to the interests of the state,

the direction of personal life
  by authority and state control.

I see people half asleep,
  half listening to half truths,

not daring to step out of line
  for fear of confrontation.

State Power

As the power of the state increases
personal freedom passes away.

As the state assumes its own identity
it ceases to exist for the people.

As the nations grow more complex year by year,
so the status of man declines.

As nations pursue their secular ways,
so men depart from their commitment to truth.

The state rules every aspect of life;
from its clutches none shall escape.

The state has become a god:
on behalf of the people it destroys the people.

State of Affairs

Low long before the state decides who shall be born,
in the name of social welfare?

How long before the state decides what we shall learn,
in the name of social ideals?

How long before the state decides who shall marry,
in the name of social justice?

How long before the state decides who shall die,
in the name of social science?

Not long in this land
before this shall come to pass:

not long before officials control our lives,
the state being their helper.

Welfare State

How many nations have lost their nerve
and allowed their freedom to be destroyed –

nations of insensitive dullards
lulled to sleep by the mother state,

encouraged by politicians
and engineers of social behaviour

who take responsibility for our lives
and penetrate the depths of our weakness!

As meddlesome men intrude in other men's affairs
so the state interferes in private life.

Each becomes his brother's keeper
and watches him from behind a door.

Children of tender years are brought to court
to be told they have been adopted.

Family life is a property of state,
valued in the courts of justice.

How can a nation preserve her integrity
when her family ties are broken?

How can people survive and flourish
when they are robbed of the freedom to be?

Worship of the Collective

Say this to those who extol the collective
and raise it above the worship of God.

What is the merit of the collective
if liberty is denied to the soul?

What is the advantage of a majority vote
if it leads a nation to ruin?

An unworthy collective will bring its own downfall,
yet who can decide the worth of a group?

A collective behaves no more wisely
than a single human being;

a collective of selfish people
will collapse at the centre.

A collective without ideals
will flounder in confusion;

a collective that has lost its hope
will bring desolation to the human soul.

How can one restore the collective
and bring about a change of heart?

Upon this question
depends the future of the world.

A Liberal Democracy

This is a warning to deprived nations.
Do you wish to become like the west –

countries with no living soul,
  industrialised and robbed of vitality,

standardised and without freedom,
  ruled by regulation and law?

If you commit yourselves to development
  you are bound to enter endless gloom.

Surrounded by vast structures of concrete,
  enveloped in systems grey and cold,

objective, materialist and standard
  you will be reduced to statistical facts.

It is better to die in one's body
  than to exist as a soulless particular.

These words come from the west –
  there is no hope in the machine.

— VIII —

THE RULE
OF LAW

An Attitude to Life

I see men laugh at the downfall of others;
   they rejoice at the plight of the weak.

I hear men scorn traditional virtues
   and lose themselves in ideas of folly.

I feel that men have lost their way
   but they refuse to acknowledge their wrong.

My heart sinks with weariness,
   my legs grow weak and fail;

my mouth will not open wide with joy
   nor my eyes shine with hope,

for the die has been cast,
   plans for the future are unrolled.

Laws that govern the universe
   also take account of man;

these laws have been ignored –
   man must take the consequences.

The Field of Runnymede

Is this the nation that received the Magna Carta?
  Is this the people who gave Shakespeare a home?

Have we a history of kings and queens,
  of noble blood and royal birth?

Is this the country of beautiful churches
  built by the hands of devoted men?

Is this the land of poetry and song,
  of genius, boldness and mirth?

Is this the land where tradition grew
  and romance flourished in every mind,

where loyalty lived in the common heart
  and respect resided in the home?

Can this be the fountain of liberty and truth,
  where the state defends the rights of all?

Is this the England of former years,
  inspired by faith and true to mankind?

Laws of England

It is plain for the world to see
    that England is a forsaken country;

it is written on the walls of cities
    that she has given up her soul.

Her laws reveal her despair;
    they legislate against our freedom.

Care has become state protection
    from the natural laws of life.

Each part of life is given a law;
    we are protected from ourselves:

there is a law for men and a law for women,
    there is a law for children's rights;

where men fall there is a law
    and where they dispute,

where men rise there is a law
    and where they agree.

There is a law against class distinction,
    bringing nonsense to human life,

paralysing those with resource and flair
    who could restore the nation to more glorious ways;

a law in favour of those who break the law,
  making the law ridiculous;

a law to confuse laws in people's minds,
  and a law that the law should be law.

There is a law to end the beginning
  before a life is born;

there will be laws to begin the end
  when a life grows old.

There are laws that reduce man to zero
  and turn his dignity to naught,

laws that crush the human soul
  like a flower beneath marching feet.

A law exists for every person in the land –
  we have exchanged our love for laws.

Every law marks the loss of freedom;
  each law indicates the state of our land.

Men everywhere say it is plain to see
  England is a forsaken country;

her laws are written on the walls of cities,
  she has given up her soul.

Death will come by law,
  desolation from decree.

On Compulsion

How can a nation enforce toleration
or compel a people to be free?

How can moderation be a rule of law
or duty be enshrined by decree?

How can a man be loyal to order
or love his neighbour against his will?

When religion disappears from the hearts of men
the character of the nation will fade away.

When men cease to exercise their will
the end is in sight for the land.

— IX —

MOTHER OF PARLIAMENTS

Publicum Consilium

I visited the House of Commons
and there saw the signs of decay –

a House split asunder by argument,
each party accusing others of mistakes.

I witness the movement of atheism
based on thoughtless ideals:

politics controlling the population,
humans locked into despair;

families moved to tower blocks,
condemned to a desolate world,

imprisoned in their cubicles
by a soulless generation.

The Ruling Class

There are those who justify their power
and there are those who do the work;

there are those who talk from platforms
and there are those who struggle to survive.

There are those who play at politics
as the people stand in the cold;

there are those with the great ideas
and there are those who are their pawns.

Resolutions, committees and rules,
meetings, motions and shows of hands;

books, programmes and interviews
as the chance to win recedes;

conferences, commissions and debates
as the reality slips away.

O for a return to leadership
that stands for the truth and stands!

Homo Popularis

Does democracy stand for privilege,
or for freedom, justice and truth?

A democracy that adjusts to power
is one that will lose its strength.

A democracy that overtakes the individual
is one that chokes the nation's health.

A democracy that interferes in private life
will remove the motive to survive.

A democracy that removes freedom of choice
is one that stops the nation's heart.

A democracy that seeks to control all
will eventually be controlled by others.

But some people are beguiled,
saying here is a solution;

they are impressed by ways like these
and vote for those who propound them.

Form of Administration

Britain is ruled from the desk
in every aspect of life.

Officials clamour and strive
to stamp their mark on the nation's soul.

There are more office workers in the ministry
than farmers working on the land.

There are more civil servants in Whitehall
than sailors on the high seas.

There are more bureaucrats in education
than teachers in the schools.

There are more paper men in industry
than workers on the factory floor.

Thus bureaucracy takes control of the mind
and is subject to its own criteria.

But do we require their management by objectives,
these experts in efficiency and method?

The Voice of the People

We do not desire the arguments
of those who impose their will on the world,

who print more money for us all
and circulate it throughout the land,

whose affairs lead to disorder
and rob a man of an honest day's work,

who take a penny off bread and put it on light
and pay for ideals through higher taxation,

who provide for the loafer and the dodger
and the one who avoids the law,

who take away our freehold and homes
and destroy the voice of independence.

No, we do not need political solutions
to the problems they have created.

We ask for honesty in those who rule,
and humility in those who lead.

The Fall of Idols

This is the end of the grand experiment –
communists and capitalists have had their day.

Their ideologies have torn the world apart
and ripped open the hearts of the nations.

They replace human initiative to do good
by bureaucracies of menacing power,

taking away the gospel of responsibility,
putting rules and regulations in its place,

confining life to administration,
nationalising or monopolising personal wealth.

Their schemes for mass development
have ignored human dignity and love.

They have brought confusion
to traditions and values

and reduced the people
to factors of need.

— X —

ELEGY
FOR ENGLAND

A Modern Civilisation

I see the charred effects of civilisation,
palpable presence of desire:

a wilderness with no soul –
humans lost in the dim lit spaces;

people sent under the ground
below the confusion and noise of the city machine,

and on people's faces
marks of weariness, tales of woe.

Elegy

Where has the character of England gone?
What has happened to the English mind?

Where now is the English way of life?
    Where are the glories of this land?

Corrupted in the path of bigotry!
    Lost in the wake of alien ideals –

ideals foreign to these shores,
    imported by consent!

Laughed at by our detractors,
    applauded by our enemies,

pitied by smaller nations in the world,
    sadly watched by our friends abroad!

The System

How it grieves me in my bones
to point to our faults when I long to praise!

How this nation tears me apart
when I look for the good and find none!

The British system has had a stroke
brought about by arterial disease,

by atheists of the modern world
who tamper and tinker in every sphere,

whose actions are like concrete –
flat, grey and uninspiring,

whose task is the erosion of loveliness –
a lowering of standards in the fight to survive.

According to Plan

There is a place of beauty –
    let us destroy it!

Here is a road –
    let us extend it!

There is a field –
    let us fill it with concrete!

There is a dwelling –
    let us demolish it!

Here is a village –
    let us make it a town!

There is a thing of antiquity –
    let us sell it abroad!

Here is a thing of weakness –
    let us exercise power!

Here is a bargain –
    let us make a profit!

We are employed to serve you faithfully,
    we are here to be obediently yours:

we will take your rates and your taxes
    and give you security of a tenuous kind.

Lament

O this nation that has lost her way
and put her trust in the hands of men,

swinging like a broken pendulum
whose weights have been smashed!

This land is a spectacle of sadness.
Men do not walk – only their shadows.

Men dare not think aloud:
they are watched and reported.

Little wonder that we flee to Europe
to be rescued from ourselves;

but here is no solution to our ills –
it will merely delay the coming of the end.

— XI —

THE ESTABLISHED CHURCH

A Secularised Church

I see a church wasting her time,
  detained in vain to the office desk;

devoted to stewardship procedures
  and striving to maintain the right connections;

indifferent to innocent lives,
  desperate to collect prestigious names;

insensitive to people and the arts,
  replete with ignorance of everyday life;

squabbling over petty issues
  that bring religion into disgrace;

impotent to preach the Gospel,
  embarrassed by the mention of Christ.

I see churches fighting wars,
  breathing hatred upon mankind;

false religions preaching a tribal god
  in place of the God of Life;

churches that treat God with familiarity
  and remove a sense of awe;

religions that abuse the nature of God
  by taking his name in vain.

Leadership

They who have risen to positions of power
   say yes to everything.

People who occupy high places
   look for comfort in the popular voice;

they prefer to smooth over every problem
   as the judgement stands at hand.

The church refuses to denounce or condemn,
   or face the nations with the truth.

The church refuses to encourage
   those who look for hope.

She betrays her privileges and benefits,
   selling her history to a clamouring world;

she hands her heritage to the state
   and loses herself in internal disputes.

The Gospel in the context of grace
   has become a theory in the name of the state.

But the ways of the world are not the ways of God.
   The world is not equal to God.

A Servant Church?

The poor do not provide the church with income,
the downtrodden are not statistically sound.

The lowly will not keep the building up
nor enable the roof to be repaired.

The ignorant will not pay the quota,
the aged will not cut the grass.

The infirm will not read the lessons,
the deprived will not provide the fees.

Why enter the homes of the poor
if the rich provide the church's funds?

A church whose god is finance
does not need to serve the poor!

A church whose statistics are important
will not attend to the slow in heart!

Why then distort the purpose of the church
by seeking first the kingdom of God?

Why seek the Spirit and the truth
when buildings serve the church's need?

A Question of Decline

Is the church a tool of state,
or a part of government rule?

Is the church to become an industry
with monopolies and boards of finance?

Is the church to be an experiment
for philosophising in verbal clichés?

Is the church to become a theatrical prop
to provide the bored with entertainment?

Is religion a drug for the people –
a sop for the masses in the land?

Is the church a means of exclusion –
a career, a trade or a private club?

Is religion a business institution,
to be run on the most efficient lines?

Is the church to bow before mammon
and yield her rights to a secular world?

Requiem for Church and State (1)

Let the church lose her identity
and be supported by the state!

Let the church become a committee,
ruled by finance and law!

Let the church continue to play safe
and disappear like a pleasant dream!

Let the church baptise all and sundry
without commitment, loyalty or faith!

Let the church continue to play the fool,
pretending that all men are Christian!

Let the church forgo the religion of poets
and give her soul to prosaic minds!

Let the church bury herself in the past
and be covered by the dust of progress!

Do we shake with horror at such things?
That is where we are drifting so aimlessly.

— XII —

TRAHISON DES CLERCS

Holy Orders

I robed with clergy who were proud of their worldliness,
strained with false sanctity in each other's churches;

clergy gathering together like sheep,
bleating and braying as lambs,

pretending they were moving forwards
by throwing away the past;

interpreting truths as it suited them
where once men stood and died;

looking inwards at their committee meetings,
subjecting care to the voice of caution.

I saw clergy who were ambitious to get on,
treating the church as a career –

unworthy men jockeying for position,
using the church as a personal tool,

stultifying reason and new ideas
against a background of sinister power.

And humbly I was stricken with grief,
bowed low in this institution cut off from God,

but determined to voice my complaint
and speak to the churches.

Cure of Souls

Parsons of parishes have turned their thoughts
    away from the people of the land.

From their lips religious words are spoken;
    they say their prayers on rare occasion.

Bishops seek their own publicity
    in television and the printed word.

Clergy in office of high order
    do not remember their calling from God,

and the words they spoke at ordination
    are forgotten without remembrance.

What are they doing with God's time?
    Where is their religious purpose in life?

The altar has become a decoration,
    the collection is counted before the people.

The Lord God Almighty once opened their minds;
    they turned to themselves and lost their vision.

He called them to serve from all walks of life,
    they responded and did not question him;

then the ways of the world overtook them,
    for committees they forsook their vocation.

On Being Relevant

Where is the Word to be heard in the churches?
Who can hear prophecies of truth?

Where are the preachers to this fallen race?
Who will declare the truth in our midst?

Not I, says the one immersed in psychology;
nor I, says the one engaged in social work.

Not I, says the one absorbed by trade unions;
nor I, says the one who is secure.

Not I, says the one who is anxious to please;
nor I, says the one who depends on goodwill.

Not I, says the one who is building his image;
nor I, says the one with his eye on the press.

Not I, says the one who serves on committees;
nor I, says the one under synodical rule.

Not I, says the one with a full diary,
rushing about to no avail.

As religion becomes more unified
so organisation takes a hold of man.

As material man is the criterion of success
so the worldly priest is rewarded by his church.

The Prospects of Success

The priest who looks first to finance
is accorded promotion and praise;

the priest who ministers to the downtrodden
is passed by on the road to success.

The priest who deals only in administration
receives recognition from the church;

the priest who is patient and kind
is the one who is treated with contempt.

The priest who speaks well in synod
is the man who catches the bishop's eye;

the priest who talks little and loves much
receives no respect from a worldly church.

The priest whose name appears in print
is the man who reads the bishop's mind;

the priest who puts first the Spirit
is persecuted in all his ways.

How else can this be in this material age
when a priest is judged by statistical returns?

Of what point is life in the Spirit
which concentrates on the kingdom of God?

Requiem for Church and State (2)

Let the state bury the dead
and the church fade like ashes in the night!

Let the state take control of marriage
and the clergy watch from the nave!

Let the state take care of our records
and leave vestries empty and bare!

Let the state buy our beautiful churches
and the clergy become their caretakers!

Let the state preach the gospel of social comfort
and teach atheism to our children in schools!

Let the state confuse Christ with other religions
and say there is no difference between them!

Let the state mix religious beliefs together
and accuse the church of prejudice!

Let the state force the church into indifference
and banish the Gospel from the land!

Where religion fails to convince by love
the state will seek to impose her laws.

Where the people are not brought to God
the state will dominate their souls.

— XIII —

APOCALYPSE

Last Supper

I went out to dinner with friends
  but remained unsatisfied.

Surrounded by imminent chaos
  we drank and gorged and laughed;

in the face of national disaster
  people were stupefied with wine.

We talked above the crystal glasses
  and the cutlery which covered the table;

the conversation was empty and void,
  the scene left me cold and confused.

Enough of this pretension,
  these habits of easy living!

The smooth talk and soft lights
  ground harsher than a rusting wheel.

Suddenly the room was filled with ghosts.
  I was revolted by the sight of them.

I felt as one alone
  to flee into the night

leaving the world behind
  chattering to the end.

Armageddon

I grow angry and burn with rage;
 a fire burns in my head.

I fume with indignation
 and curse this stupid world.

Men are trapped by their ingenious schemes
 and caught in the grip of their inventions.

The subtleties of their minds confuse them,
 the panic of their hearts condemns.

The bones of men twist and bend,
 they burn with the pain of fire.

The human frame is racked with disease,
 the mind of man imagines evil things.

Suspicion breeds in the heart of man
 and doubt turns into cynical despair.

Mistrust fills the soul of man
 and poisons the fibres of his being.

Jealousy swells the eyes of man
 and brings about his moral decay.

Man is torn from his roots and cast aside
 because he is no longer fit to live.

Dies Irae, Dies Illa

How long before it happens?
How long before the end?

We move forwards into the fire,
 judged at every step we take.

I shout and shake my fists
 at the fate of this forsaken world,

but men are proud of their folly
 and scoff at the warnings of doom.

They snigger at words such as these
 and say here are reactionary words.

But wait for the reaction of God –
 it is coming like a mighty storm.

See, the day of collapse is near!
 The time of death is upon us!

Draw near to the death bed of the nations –
 hear the last choking breath of life!

Destruction awaits us like a monstrous death;
 ruin attends us like a digger of graves.

The gates of death are opened up –
 they slope to the furnace of hell.

The End of the Age

If the nations continue in their ways
  these words will be fulfilled.

Men will laugh at these predictions
  but not when they come to pass.

The familiar routine of order
  will give way to sinister rule;

the social state will lie in ruins
  and complaints will be heard no more.

Men will starve in the open streets –
  streets once full of affluent splendour;

neon lights of western abundance
  will be extinguished once and for all.

Collections of selfish men
  will behave like a jungle of savages;

they will snarl and growl at each other
  and destroy in order to survive.

Families will fight for themselves in the towns
  and flee for their safety to the fields.

Tools of commerce will be rendered useless
  and negotiations shall be completely irrelevant.

Vision of the Final Days

Wrath pours from seven bowls,
mountains are drenched in blood.

The machine and the stock exchange
shall barter no more.

Justice shall turn to wormwood;
flesh and wood rot shall not be.

Forget! they cry. Forget
the desire of thy memorial name!

For objects of speculation
are now only probable

and the method only relative.
In the season of the spring rain

man's desire to be lovable
is merely desire for fame.

The Apocalypse

The moon is turned to blood,
the orb is black as cloth.

In their possible courses
stars tumble and fall.

Fig trees shed their autumn fruit
at the rise of the winter gale.

Man calls to the mountains
but the hills are a delusion;

stones and rock are among them
and the rose fades.

At the rise of the shaft smoke
father will rise against son.

Calamity and issue,
sulphur and fire.

—— XIV ——

LAMENTATIONS

Burial Ground

Standing in the grass,
  staring at the wind,

I look at the town
  deep in this present,

infinitesimal point of reference
  for memorials of times past.

No possession fills the mind.
  The flowers at the roadside

cannot grasp the meaning,
  do not understand the rhyme.

Black stones inscribe to memory
  images of people never seen,

in their homes or in the streets,
  departed from this order in time.

Silence of Death

Soul urges for a meaning to it all,
ruminating silently the winters past.

Rotting corpses in the grave,
reaching to beauty through decay.

Self within self is not found,
element dissociated from the ground,

crude snap fallen short of the oak leaf,
all our life in the cemetricious quiet,

generation of all things visibly born,
from elements compounded remain so.

Descent into Hell

Peering into nature,
to the depths of the marrow,

I see the death of soul,
desolation at the roots of Babel.

I stare past the elm trees,
chilled in the city frost.

Finitude explores infinity
in the shallow grave.

Between the clutterless branches
whines the wind,

always present on the park bench
in the empty evening light.

Requiescat In Pace

I have read Lucretius
and of Democritus,

who told their tale
to the atomic school;

who said, concerning matter,
it is ultimately discontinuous.

And when the sun rose
I did agree:

we all believe,
but only to the end.

Act of Remembrance

This is a time of death and despair;
communicating lines are broken.

We remember who has gone before,
thereby attempt to conquer time.

The wind cuts clean like a knife,
bleeding the briar and the thorn.

Thou given life in the tumulus sod
rests in dampness and death and God.

THE CALL

Prayer of Rage

O God, why do you let the days pass by?
My fear and fury consume me!

Men with hard heads consult each other
and bring us nearer to disaster.

Men with jealous eyes watch each other
but they are unable to see the truth.

Men with stiff necks judge each other
as the world disintegrates around them.

Why do you not act, O God?
Are you blind to our deeds?

How is it that the wicked achieve success
when the innocent are crushed underfoot?

How is it that noisy men prosper
while the quiet man suffers wrong?

Nations who commit horrible crimes
abound in their wealth and arrogance.

Surely this destroys the sense of justice
and breaks the laws of truth?

God arise and prove your honour!
Justify the righteous in their ways!

The Laws of Destiny

The voice of God came to me, saying:
Go, prophesy to the nations,

to people of plenty but in need,
a world of promise yet forsaken.

Speak to those with no foundation,
who refute the vision of truth;

to those who will not hear the truth
and refuse to mend their ways;

to people who have lost their nerve
and allowed their freedom to be destroyed,

who give away their inheritance
to appease the fashionable mind.

Do not be afraid of their reaction
nor use words that strive to please,

for these are people with stubborn hearts,
cynical and senseless people –

a generation that prefers to be deceived
for the sake of comfort and ease of mind;

a world of materialists and unbelievers
who scorn attempts to convert them.

Prayer of Contrition

O Lord my God,
how can I obey your command?

I am confronted by the nature of sin;
there is no peace in my heart.

I dread the world by day
and the company of friends at night;

the evil I wish to avoid
is always present in my life.

I am the victim of circumstance,
no right prevails in my thought;

I am caught in the trap of modern ways
and surrounded by whirlpools of chaos.

Truly the time has come upon us
in this socially contrived existence

to rouse ourselves from our slumbers
and return to the source of life.

But how dare I speak to your people,
so conscious am I of my own faults?

Who am I that I should speak,
or call the nations to repent?

A Call to Prophesy

You may object but I have chosen you.
You cannot refuse me, said the Lord.

I have revealed my intentions
  and made my will known.

I have confidence in you
  though you have lost your trust in me;

I have called you,
  I will never let you down.

After a drought in creative activity
  you will burst into poetry and song.

After years of doubt and hardship
  your life will be restored.

Why do you draw back in disbelief
  and withhold your trust from what is revealed?

It is the purpose of the prophet in the world
  to disclose to his people the mind of God.

Will you turn again and accept your vocation?
  Will you burn again with the Word in your heart?

Will you believe in the mysteries of being
  or succumb to the spirit of the age?

Prayer of Doubt

But of all the created universe, O God,
    why are you concerned with the earth?

Why do you focus on this corner in space,
    this insignificant point of no magnitude?

When I consider the millions of worlds
    scattered as dust in an infinite void,

the great depths of the inner regions
    opening new dimensions of life,

the great sweep of time over billions of years
    making our generation but an instant in history,

I ask how was it all created, why is it here?
    Where are we from and where shall we go?

Why are you concerned, O God?
    Why are you troubled with man?

Life Assurance

Let us come together, said the Lord,
in the battle for the human soul.

I made man to live for ever
but he does not hear the news.

I have in store the richest blessing,
but where is man to be found?

I have called you to this office
and require that you should serve.

Do not be overawed by articulate men
but stand firm by your faith in God.

Do not lose heart by your mistakes
nor forget the Lord in your distress.

When prophecy declares the truth
how can the voice be ignored?

When prophecy speaks of things to come
how can one doubt the inspiration?

Confront the people with their folly
and the results of their evil deeds.

Stand and speak to the nations.
Say – This is the word of the Lord!

LETTERS
TO A FRACTURED
SOCIETY

— I —

TO THE
NATIONS

To Humankind

You have heard, you have known,
you have had God's ways set before you.

You indulge yourselves in evil;
your institutions are in decay.

Examine yourselves in your assemblies,
look to yourselves in your homes.

Say to your souls – are we truly content?
Surely the answer is No!

You know this yet you pursue destruction,
so you shall be given to your ways.

You deserve only ruin and shame;
peace is no longer yours.

Each says in his pride
it is my neighbour,

he is wrong, he is to blame,
he it is who brings destruction.

But you are all guilty in your hearts,
and you shall be judged according to law

for testing the truth by the mood of the times,
according to opinion and fashion.

A Question of Priorities

I speak to men and women with small minds –
minds closed and devoid of vision,

limited to immediate requirements,
    confined to things they do not understand –

who do not know where they are going
    as they wander down their empty paths,

who scorn the traditional mind
    and readily accept the latest trend.

Why do you bend the rule of law
    for the sake of political expedients?

Why do you pay homage to evil forces
    for the sake of temporary peace?

Why do you refuse to be concerned
    as the loud mouthed get their way?

Why do you allow the competent voice
    to be drowned by inarticulate roars?

Men everywhere are blind to what is happening,
    deaf to the events around them –

they drift into a world of terror and ruin;
    they slowly drift to the end.

The End of Democracy

I speak to nations who pretend to be democratic
in service to the needs of self;

to governments who fail to serve the people
and become instruments to betray their trust;

to states who rebuff personal initiative
and choke to death all inspiration;

to politicians of the world
who clamour to organise man's greed;

to lawyers who break the law
and law makers who refuse to obey;

to churches who abuse their privilege
and engage in worldly pursuit.

You who have such slick answers to life,
whose hearts are swamps of self concern:

here is the cause of your decline,
here is the reason for your decay.

You imagine easy paths to success
and take short cuts to the courts of ruin,

but your world revolves round power
and such power leads only to death!

An Apostate Age

What is wrong with you, my people?
Why has your spirit turned to dust?

Why do the hills no longer rejoice
   nor the streets shout with joy?

A terrible thing has happened in the world.
   Man has turned away from God!

Truly you have turned from God
   and find no meaning in his name.

O you Godless men and women,
   who have no substance in your lives:

what is the present object of worship,
   the latest design to hold you in awe?

Your lives have been dissected
   by atheists with political minds.

You worship false images and idols,
   money, esteem and material goods.

Little wonder that the earth is in ruins
   as you wander about in a state of decay.

Your gods are no greater than blocks of stone.
   They change as the seasons from year to year.

To Leaders of the Nations

You leaders of church and state
and all engaged in public work.

This is a word to you,
to those who have set the pace.

How you could inspire the world
with integrity, justice and vision!

How you could restore the future
by encouraging a sense of hope!

The road back is hard and long –
who is prepared to take it?

The way ahead is full of trouble –
who will accept the challenge?

Who will set out in faith,
in purity, peace and love?

Those in positions of power
must provide the lead.

Where is there a voice to be heard –
a common voice for the people?

Is it in the unions or in industry?
Is it in government or the church?

— II —

TO CHURCHES, TEMPLES
AND SYNAGOGUES

The Wrong Direction

Say this to the Church of England –
your priests are devoid of purpose.

Say this to the Church of Rome –
authority is not yours.

Say this to the Free Churches –
your name is no longer free.

You are studious for effect
but indifferent to cause.

Ministers bend over backwards
to show they are no different.

Bishops affirm the status quo;
they have folded the garment of truth.

The prophet has lost his voice,
the words of God are no longer heard.

The layman is dismayed and confused,
watching in vain for signs of hope.

It is my love for the church
that causes these words to be spoken.

It is because of my love for the soul
that these words come straight from my heart.

To Lukewarm Churches

You were chosen as instruments of peace
but you turn out to be vehicles of chaos.

On your shoulders God set the office of hope
but you have plundered and talked only waste.

Some have pondered for far too long,
unable to decide what to do;

others agree with the strongest voice,
afraid to stand alone for the truth.

You have become a mark of mistrust,
closing down the intelligent mind.

You concede as the state takes over
and idly watch as freedom disappears.

You who bureaucratise unity
to create a uniform church:

when bureaucracy controls your faith
there is no religion in the land.

Now you will discover the power of evil
as innocents are lost in a cruel world.

For all time you shall see the folly of your ways,
the foolishness of your adjustments to fashion.

An Age of Committees

Synods and councils of churches,
and all engaged in authority and rule.

You forgo the Spirit for the ways of men,
giving up prayer for the conference table.

You think that resolutions at a meeting
will fulfil the needs of the people.

You believe that a majority vote
is an indication of the will of God.

How wrong you are;
how stupid you have become.

Whoever heard of a committee or synod
that failed to centralise its power?

When a clear decision is made
be sure no committee is present.

Does a committee create a work of art?
It merely consumes the people's time.

Obduracy is bred on committees;
in them compromise is born.

Invention is the mother of achievement
but committees simply crush ideas.

Thanks to a Synodical Church...

For creating a commercial religion
governed by annual returns.

For centralising the administration,
increasing the administrative load.

For engaging the church in trivia
and leading her into schism.

For investing her money in commerce
and her soul in the markets of change.

For closing down places of worship
and putting them up for sale.

For converting chapels into warehouses
to store the goods of the world.

What use now are your diocesan boards,
your repairs and drainpipes and halls?

What use now the sale of your rectories,
your land, endowments and glebe?

You raise quota to pay for your schemes,
taxing parishioners beyond their means,

but I will lay waste your churches
and make barren your plans, says God.

Parochial Pejoratives

God is not pleased with you parishioners
who close your minds to the purpose of love,

who expect the services of the church
yet find neither time nor money to keep her;

who never darken her doors
to engage in private prayer,

who do nothing to maintain her buildings
yet complain when they are closed down.

And you bigoted fussers and meddlers
who see only regulations and rules,

who demand all and give nothing
and have the clergy running after you:

you resort to seeking power
and work for personal esteem;

you nod and wink at council meetings
and plot and scheme but fail to build.

Change your ways
and serve a world in need,

or leave the church altogether
and let others get on with the job.

To Church of England Parties

You middle of the road churchgoers,
   causing havoc down the highway of life.

You precious high church people,
   bowing and burning incense in vain.

You evangelicals with wealthy backgrounds,
   uttering platitudes for the poor.

You who cause spiritual divisions
   by organising religion on party lines,

who pounce on the mistakes of others
   and proudly sound your voice of judgement.

You have failed to make your judgements true
   but by God you shall be judged.

You smooth talking theologians with vague ideas
   and weak kneed ordinands at your feet,

searching the current theme in theology
   in which to construct a liturgical mould:

you claim to hold the answer to life
   but mystery remains with the kingdom of God.

You cannot reach its depths.
   The mind of God cannot be known.

To False Liberals

This is to a church immersed in atheism,
indifferent to her religious call,

in which children are baptised without meaning
and people attend church without cause.

Prepare for a time of sorrow
when the Word appears to come to naught,

when your pews stand empty and ignored
and the state takes over your work.

Look to the future without your comforts,
when the people reject your words and deeds;

when governments convert your children
and parents are confirmed into political rules;

when the church is ruled by ignorance
and ceases to be the home of truth;

when the shepherd is led by the flock
and all becomes lost.

Is this too ridiculous to imagine?
I see it happening, says the Lord.

If you continue with your arrogant pose
much worse will befall you.

To Evangelicals

As you proliferate day by day
you increase in number but not in spirit.

You pride yourselves in your relevance
by adopting a contemporary style.

You who look for quick results
and boast of large congregations,

who speak of growing churches –
see where they are when you have gone.

You are uprooted from your traditions,
but do you speak to the modern age?

No! You have failed in your task,
mesmerised by the secular mind.

Where is the beauty of your religion,
the inspiration behind your faith?

Where is your vision of peace and worship,
and the power of your spiritual lives?

I will cast you from my sight
and know you no more, says God.

I will set up the real church;
you will not stand in my way.

To Radicals

Religion has a mystical foundation;
  it cannot be defined by councils and creeds:

do not place your whole trust in reason,
  but seek a balance between logic and faith.

Religion is no department of science:
  do not be allured by techniques;

do not be led astray by modish thought
  nor allow despair to be your constant guide.

Be watchful of those who speak softly
  but create a church of confusion and doom,

of those who seek to change society
  but betray the freedom of the age.

Be on your guard against cynical minds
  who seek to explain the truth away;

they are found in theological circles
  as well as the atheist's fold.

Realism is found in the Scriptures –
  a fashion contrary to modern trends.

Read again the Gospel of God.
  There lies the answer to your need.

To Traditionalists

To the people of the churches
and synagogues and temples of God.

You are citizens of two kingdoms –
one in earth and one in heaven.

Weigh the scales of justice and love:
they will find a balance in truth.

Measure the rule of law and habit:
its limit is the grave.

Have done with your double standards!
You are to proclaim – not to conform.

Listen to the humblest voice
and do not surround yourselves with power.

You who expect much of your priests:
make prayer commensurate with expectation.

Let your worship be enriched by the arts,
and your liturgies alive with the Spirit.

Where is your fellowship of love?
It must be known and preached.

Where is your theology of prayer?
It must be lived!

To Christians

This is a time for endurance and work,
a time for resolution and faith.

This is a time to turn again to God,
to put him before the world.

Bring the Gospel to your cities
and renew the heart within decay.

Bring the Gospel to the dirt and grime,
to the lowliest places in your towns.

Bring the Gospel to rural life,
to the farms and cottages of the land.

Bring the Gospel to the market place,
into the springs and streams of life.

Bring the Gospel to the workbench,
to the production line and canteen.

Bring the Gospel to the industrial floor,
to the boardroom and shareholders' meeting.

Bring the Gospel to the stock exchange,
to the hard hitting places of financial stress.

Bring the Gospel to parliaments,
where decisions are made for your lives.

To World Religions

To religions at ease in the west
and all who wish to be popular.

To religions at war in the east
and those who exercise intolerance.

To religions that have caused such havoc
but refuse to give up their power.

To all who attend the sacred House
and claim to worship God.

Guilt pervades the mind of man
though each one deflects the blame.

The absence of God dispossesses man
and dislocates his reason to be.

Let your churches become sanctuaries of prayer
to guard the rights of the people.

Let your councils be repositories of grace
to inspire others to experience God.

Let your synods be guardians of peace,
equality, liberty and truth.

Let the centre of your lives be changed
and you will live in freedom from self.

— III —

TO THE
CLERGY

To Inferior Clergy

You priests of the House of God
who are as dull as you could possibly be.

You intone your services with pained expression;
you pander to the rich and rush to greet them.

You lack the note of authority;
you are too concerned with your status –

desperate to buy the latest liturgy
or to discover the most recent trend;

anxiously hiding behind your traditions,
using them as a cloak to hide your fear –

each one busier than the next man
with no time for anyone:

clerical grey suits and clerical minds,
stuffy, pompous, self righteous people

with not a word of hope for humankind,
not a whisper of salvation.

Therefore, because of your apostasy,
the nations have plunged towards ruin.

You have failed to enter the world
but the world has entered you.

To Boring Preachers

You are charged to preach the Word of God
and give pastoral care to the people,

but your churches have been desecrated
because few of the clergy are spiritually born.

You recite your words week by week
yet you do not know me, says God;

you speak down to the people in pews
but you do not know them, says God.

People are starved of spiritual direction
while you work out your roles at conferences.

You restore the confession to your worship
and repeat your faults again and again.

O lead the world into repentance
by first repenting yourselves!

Whatever you preach in the pulpit
must first be lived in your lives.

Joy is no intellectual construction,
eternal life no academic idea.

Your task is not to adjust to society
but to point the soul to the kingdom of heaven.

To Preferred Clergy

You deans and provosts of cathedrals,
responsible for the House of Prayer.

You say our churches are empty and ignored –
how shall we fill them in this modern age?

Let us organise carnivals and festivals;
let us invite politicians to argue in the nave.

Let us invite tourists to stand and gape
and file noisily round the aisles.

Let us turn our cathedrals into money centres,
cafeterias, cinemas and entertainment halls.

Let us pander to the masses
and ignore spiritual beauty and truth.

Why not let your cathedrals crumble into decay
if that is the attitude of the people to worship?

Why invent false means to keep them going
if their purpose is forgotten by an ignorant state?

This is what I say
in reply to your foolish ways:

I will grind your schemes into dust
and cast them to the winds, says God.

The Ordinal

Here is a message to you bishops,
who are consecrated to do God's work.

Do your churches lack people to serve?
Take the leaders from your pews and stalls!

Are you short of apostles and prophets?
Ordain them where they are!

Why join your parishes together
when leaders are there in your midst?

Treat boards of selection with caution,
accept those who measure to the call;

lay hands on the pure and simple hearted,
those who are set apart by God.

Look again at your theological colleges,
which teach men to be critical of the Word

and encourage scepticism and disbelief
in the smooth pursuit of rational truth.

Have done with your industrial management
and techniques from a temporal stage;

these are days of urgent need –
you are moving into the age of prophecy.

A Pastoral Charge

Hear this, you church dignitaries
who are charged to guard the fold.

Enough of this tinkering with liturgies,
of meeting behind doors in your churches.

Enough of the neglect of your ministries
and ignorance of the needs of the people,

of minutes and resolutions and agendas,
of consultations and conversations.

Enough of aimless wanderings down byways –
get to work each one of you!

Leave your committees and meetings;
care for your people with love.

Tend the sheep and the shepherds;
look for those who are lost.

Be tender hearted to those who err
and denounce the wicked at heart.

Especially care for the young,
for those with sensitive minds.

Be fathers to your flocks and their pastors;
let your love be of God and true.

The Gospel to Proclaim

Clergy and ministers of God's household,
you must learn to trust the Spirit of God.

Pray for the Spirit to enter your souls;
be filled with grace in your work.

Restore quietness and peace to your lives;
endure the times through which you pass.

Refuse to charge to and fro as ones who are lost;
set your task and achieve it through prayer.

Come now! Proclaim the truth with power.
Do not yield to compromise.

Where there is humbug and pretence
you must stand and speak.

The Lord God is strength in your weakness.
He has called you – be fit for the call.

He sends you into the world –
go in the power of his name.

Do not think of what you are to say;
his words are those of creation.

Do you believe this or will you hold back?
Are you with the Lord?

— IV —

TO WORLD
POLITICIANS

Political Wisdom

Is wisdom wanting in government circles?
Let humility be a rule of law!

Is wisdom lacking amongst the people?
Let them seek it with all their heart!

Wisdom guides a nation forward
by discerning the values of truth.

Wisdom grants to a people vision
to interpret the contingencies of time.

Wisdom guards the portals of freedom
against those who seek to knock them down.

A wise people will preserve its succès d'estime
and reform its life for the future.

A wise nation will use her resources shrewdly
and refuse to rush towards exhaustion.

A wise nation is one that plans with care
and allows the people to play their part.

Give wisdom to the people
and it will be given to the politician.

But what is the source of wisdom?
Where can wisdom be found?

To Power Seekers

Hear this, you ambitious politicians
who seek office at all costs,

who renounce a sacred trust,
playing to galleries of fools.

Thinking only of your own position
you have desecrated the past;

working hard for your popularity
you have nearly destroyed the future.

You politicos who argue for your security
while the world is rotting at the core:

the courage of your convictions
extends no further than your term of office.

You rabble who clamour and shout
and set the taste for vulgarity:

you speak in support of democracy –
you will bring it to an end.

Expedience, manipulation and self interest
serve only temporary pleasure.

True confidence is born of integrity,
not found in half formed ideas.

With Prejudice

You party dogmatists,
  whose opinions are already formed.

You take a high handed view of politics,
  treating minorities with contempt.

Ignorant yet self assured,
  convinced you are right in all you do,

you dismiss the wise as reactionaries
  and utter platitudes to a gullible people.

When the scheme goes wrong who is to blame?
  Others, the system, but never yourselves!

When cornered you simply quote statistics
  and point to the faults of everyone else.

You pursue your dogmas to the end
  and propogate your theories to no avail.

Reform! Be tolerant of minority views
  and do not rush to agree with your peers.

It is not sufficient to be elected to office
  by proving your opposite number wrong.

Concentrate not so much on the faults of others
  as on the purpose common to you all.

To Complacent Politicians

Here is a word to conformists
who say everything is perfectly all right,

the do-gooders and socially sublime
who see good where there is wickedness.

You say peace where there is war
and become blind to the violence around you.

You refuse to accept that evil exists
and define it away for your peace of mind.

Can you not see into the future
as you glibly set up your precedents?

Once the purpose of life is removed
man will choose the way of ease.

How tidy you make your social theories,
how slick the conclusions of your thoughts.

You face the greatest peril of all –
extinction by your own complacency.

Must indolence rule the heart
or apathy direct the brain?

Let politics and the passions
be guided by the converted soul.

To Diffident Politicians

You statesmen who lack courage
to stand and speak with authority.

Why do you lead by walking backwards,
always facing those who give their vote?

Why do you abjure your responsibilities
and dissolve them in committees?

Why do you obey the party machine
and follow the voice of patronage?

All this will not do!
Where is the proof of your worth?

Mankind is starving at its roots –
respond with urgency or it will be too late!

Have done with your tiresome meetings,
your endless procedures and rules.

Give the people the tools of freedom;
you cannot control every part of life.

Release the energies of human potential.
Remove the obstacles to personal growth.

Trust the people with their skills –
they will show you the way ahead.

Concerning Leadership

To lead requires maturity of mind
and insight into the laws of life.

The strong leader has the courage to lead
and not merely represent the people.

He stands above party spirit
and sectarian conflicts of self concern;

he refuses to be moved by personal interest,
or be influenced by corruptive powers.

A sound leader distinguishes fact from opinion
before he accedes to the will of the people;

not all the people are right all the time
but a wise leader will discern the truth.

A confident leader will not seek to please,
nor use foolish phrases and empty words;

he will not allow his word to be reduced,
nor conduct his campaigns with malice and wrath.

The leader will look first to his principles
before he embarks on political schemes;

he will not cheapen his politics
but will found them upon eternal truths.

To Leaders of States

You exist in a changing world
to which adjustment must be made.

Brace yourselves for a new dawn
and become leaders with practical hope.

The people wait for your guidance
and demand true leadership from your ranks.

It seems to be a difficult task
but with will it can be achieved.

The first and most important challenge
is for each person to consider his soul –

to see his soul in relation to God
and not merely as an entity of state.

It is wiser for a politician to be religious
than it is for religion to enter politics;

it is wiser for a leader to be religious
than it is for religion to look for a cause.

Do you try to bring peace by wisdom?
Or seek knowledge before opinions are given?

Do you seek to understand the oppressed?
Or guidance from those you consider wrong?

On Politics

Here is the purpose of politics
with meaning for this age:

to prepare wisely for the future
in the light of experience and merit.

Politics should cease to be absolute
and recognise its proper sphere,

for politics belongs to the earthly realm
and is concerned for men where they are.

A government that stands for the individual
is greater than one that merely produces schemes.

A government that cherishes the human soul
will continue to grow in strength.

A government that seeks to do right
will achieve much through honour.

A government that upholds justice
will do so in the spirit of freedom.

A government that is loved by the people
will establish liberty in the land.

A government that trusts its people
is truly a gift to the world.

Towards a True Peace

To the people of the state
and leaders of the establishment.

It is a desirable thing to do,
to disarm this savage world.

You must try with all your might
to rid the planet of war

and bring all your energies to bear
upon the problem of human survival.

It is one thing to say peace
and another to work towards it,

for, though you pray for amity,
peace is only mutually achieved.

Join in the brotherhood of man
by bestowing a beautiful freedom –

a freedom that brings with it care
and concern for your fellow men.

Look to each other to serve
in duty, trust and love –

let each one begin with himself
and the family surrounding him.

Against the Tide

The years of glib advice are over,
the days of platitudes are at an end.

You are all guilty of making mistakes;
now is the time for making good.

Increase your aid together
and show the world your care.

Reduce your spending on arms,
reduce your spending on goods.

Reduce your spending on comfort,
reduce your spending on pleasure.

Reduce your spending on homes,
reduce your spending on roads.

Reduce your spending on wealth,
reduce your spending on self.

Reduce your spending on loans
and on servicing your debts.

Return to human charity,
return to human help.

Return to brotherly love,
return to the compassion of Christ.

— V —

TO BUREAUCRATS, ACCOUNTANTS AND LAWYERS

A Common Agricultural Policy

Bureaucrats! Consider the plight of farmers –
men who have become embittered,

buying sheep for a pittance
and selling them for little more –

cattle grazing in the fields
to be slaughtered at a loss,

poverty below the windswept hills
as harvest comes to a close.

Consider those who fish at sea,
an industry corroded by regulation and law –

all the result of your policy making
which is clearly out of touch.

You say you understand but do nothing;
you allow corruption and bow to the middle man.

You create vast reserves of food
as the poor continue to starve.

Truly, yours will be a desolate earth –
a land burnt dry and without its crops,

a tool in the hands of economists,
empty of purpose, devoid of decision.

An Ordered World

Nations are controlled by bureaucrats
  who manipulate people from afar,

who never do a proper day's work
  and exist à propos de rien;

who increase from year to year,
  reporting others and supporting themselves,

who attend lunches and dinners and conferences
  to procure the attentions of image makers.

Let us argue with these smooth men
  who demand their returns by the end of the week,

who issue forms to be returned completed
  by frantic servants of public taste.

They may be members of trade unions
  or on the boards of directors;

they may be government officials
  or even on the councils of churches.

Of what use are they precisely?
  Are they not parasites who stultify growth?

Is bureaucracy the only purpose in life?
  Is social perfection the end of existence?

To Social Dogmatists

You donors to chaos and disease,
who invert the laws of common sense.

How laughable are your policies and rules.
You who counsel others – counsel yourselves!

Your inspectors snoop into personal lives
and invade private houses in organised gangs.

You are terrified of social unrest
and serve the people with half truths.

You show indifference to their spiritual needs
and train them for the welfare state

with care that is based on borrowed money
and charity on long term loans.

Here is the way to social utopia –
death of the individual.

Here is the way to equality –
remove the freedom of choice.

Here is the way to equal rights –
remove the rights of all.

This tragic way of organised man
will lead to his own destruction.

The End of the Road

Look to your ways and procedures,
you who claim statistical control

in government, trade unions and churches,
in industry, the arts and entertainment.

You have lost yourselves
under an avalanche of forms;

the urge to rule by order and routine
has stifled the fertile mind.

The skills of mankind
are wasted by budgets and plans;

the character of the people
is a grey sheet of paper.

You who sacrifice great principles
for the sake of detail and petty concern:

be warned that your efficient methods
will not bring prosperity,

for yours are nations with no purpose,
your people are people with no name.

This world once plunged into darkness
will not be rescued again.

Quo Iure?

This is a word of warning
to those who frame equivocal laws,

who operate the statutes of atheists,
unable to perceive the truth.

You work by punitive regulations
and remove the people's rights;

you take away their liberties
by turning exceptions into rules.

You advance your restrictive principles
in a clutter of unworkable laws;

you take pride in creating precedents
and stand powerless in their wake.

You absolve the guilty from wrong
and condone the breaking of God's law.

Morality has become political
and the nations degenerate.

Do you pass your acts and edicts
to justify your power?

You stubbornly go it alone,
oblivious of God and the moral code.

Prescription for Law

Where is the court of appeal
against nonsense, injustice and ridiculous laws?

Better that a man should obey from the heart
than serve under compulsion,

for justice is an attitude of soul,
not obedience to complex rules.

The laws of a land must be just
and not in favour of the few;

the laws of a land must be few
and not in favour of the rich.

Civil law must protect the people
and not be biassed towards the criminal mind.

Common law should not prescribe action
nor tell the people what to do.

Criminal law should chiefly be for guidance,
forbidding only what is wrong.

You who think that restoration of justice
requires the creation of numerous laws:

obey the laws of the constitution
but remember the greater law of God.

— VI —

TO COUNCILS, ARCHITECTS AND DEVELOPERS

To Corrupt Councillors

You councillors who meet in city halls,
joking and scoring political points.

If once you were sincere in your dealings,
certainly now you are not.

You bend the truth to suit your aim
and confuse the minds of the people;

you adjust the meaning of your words
according to your ability to lie.

If you lived in the homes of your tenants
you would perish within a week,

but your own nest is feathered well
as the people pay you to talk.

We all condemn those who live in slums
but your fate will be worse than theirs;

because you are hypocrites in power
your lives stand forever condemned.

By signing your meaningless directives
you have left your names for posterity.

The very power you so desperately seek
will be your own undoing.

To Myopic Councils

You public servants who serve yourselves,
you rulers of law and dealers in land.

You do not know where your duty lies
as you belittle your country.

You invent schemes where there are none
and create vast tracts of urban waste;

your streets are littered with human detritus
and chaos ensues where traffic prevails.

The city offers no hope to the poor,
the country no retreat for peace;

you despise the rural way of life
and displace the soul of man.

Emptiness, emptiness in your thoughts and plans;
out of touch, out of touch are your strange ideas.

Temporary, temporary are your latest designs,
passing away with each generation.

Great attributes of natural life
are slowly but surely entering decline;

so the value of life is determined
to suit a people with no foundation.

A Country Code

Do you need a country of motorways
along which to dash yourselves to pieces?

Do you need larger vehicles
to shake the ancient village?

Do you need to pull down old homes
to build houses that will not last?

Do you need tall buildings
and committees to fill them?

Do you need to borrow more money
and sell your birthright abroad?

Do you need revisions of policy
to confuse each generation born?

Do you need to destroy your churches
for the sake of temporary ideals?

Do you need to defoliate your forests
to save a crumbling economy?

How much good there is around you,
betrayed by your stubborn hearts.

This tragic way of existence
will surely lead to your decay.

To Urbanists

You who build multi million pound centres
and waste resources on idealist schemes.

You abolish reminders of tradition
and construct your images in their place.

You distort your cultural past
in the name of progress.

You make prisons out of cities
and erect barriers against human freedom.

You take away a man's home
and give him minimum compensation.

You create huge metropolitan areas,
yet speak in favour of the individual.

Enough of this public expenditure,
doubling the rates to pay for your deals!

Know what to develop and what to expand
but know also what to leave alone.

Let the artificial structures be broken
which bind men everywhere in chains.

Reduce your demand for development.
Learn to lead a simple life.

Prudens Futuri

To secular man with his advanced technology,
bringing ecological disaster to the earth.

Are your ways so necessary for the future?
Does not the state of the planet prove you void?

Consider God's plan of evolution
in the universe of his creation.

What artifice produces the wild flower
or clothes the hills with the windblown grass?

Come, let us work together with creation.
Nothing shall be lost, says Almighty God.

Material stability and spiritual growth
will bring the discovery of lasting peace.

Let culture return to the centres of cities,
and music and drama replace congestion and noise.

Let your cities be designed for people
and their institutions for human beings.

Let true freedom be known on the plains,
on the marshlands and in the fens.

Let the fields be restored to their fullness
and the hills to their former joys.

— VII —

TO
CAPITALISTS

Concerning Wealth

A nation whose strength is in capital
makes capital out of people –

thus people are used for increasing wealth
and human dignity is at risk.

Power is the rate of doing work,
it is lost when work is denied –

thus unemployment becomes a tool for despots
to create the machinery of obedience.

Wealth is power to establish rights,
it can also deny the rights of others –

thus personal riches never increase
unless somebody's somewhere diminish.

A nation that profits only the few
is one whose wealth is unfairly shared.

A nation in which people are unemployed
is one whose morale will decline.

A nation whose people cannot save
is a burden for all to see.

A nation cannot keep her wealth
if it is lost in random desire.

To Corrupt Investors

You who deal in stocks and shares
  and move your money round the globe,

distorting the face of reality
  with your data and systems and graphs.

What is your standard of life
  but material goods and increasing wealth?

What is the purpose of your investments?
  It is simply to achieve a high return.

You make nonsense of human life;
  you have had your day and are now ridiculous.

Your fiscal ideology has become rotten:
  total confusion will be the result for all.

O that my people would change their ways
  and keep economics to its proper station.

O that you would amend your lives
  and not condemn your souls to possessions.

Then perhaps you could smile again
  and relax in the presence of each other,

and talk more easily in the world
  and learn to love life as it is.

To Speculators

Is it right that you should continue to spend
and compel your children to inherit your debts?

Is it right that you should invent a market
when there is no desire for your goods?

Is it right that industry should expand
when it cannot pay a worker's wage?

Is it right that profits should go to the rich
and losses be borne by the poor?

Should not those who produce the goods
be entitled to a share in the gain?

Should not a portion of your wealth
go to those who cannot work?

Should not a percentage of your dividend
support those who cannot strike?

Must industrial development
exploit man and nature to the end?

Are you wise in your collectivism?
A single error will cause untold harm.

The root of your problem is greed.
Unless you reform there will be no end to despair.

Advice to Capitalists

Integrity in the world of finance
  is worth more than increased profits;

honesty in a competitive world
  is finer than successful shares.

You do not have to justify your existence
  by launching into expensive schemes,

for a pauper with dignity and honour
  is worth more than a rich man who is a fool.

Work hard for the sake of your future
  and reap the reward for your labour,

but remember that life has a purpose
  beyond the boundaries of profit and loss.

Happy is the man with a small income
  who loves his children and is friend of all,

but desperate the one with high return
  who destroys his home in his greed for more.

Share your wealth and possessions,
  be generous with your fellow men;

give away some of your riches
  to the desperately needy and poor.

— VIII —

TO DIRECTORS, EXECUTIVES AND MANAGERS

The Counting House

Here is a definition of inflation
for those who refuse to understand.

When a man works half time for full pay
and goods are sold at twice their worth;

when ten are employed in place of two
and two factories are built instead of one;

when production exceeds demand
and wages increase as their value declines;

when pleasure costs more than earnings supply
and debtors borrow in order to spend;

when the naïve are given rank before time
and receive honour before it is due;

when attention is paid to cheap ideas
and the wise are treated as fools;

when the voice of prejudice assumes authority
and the able mind conforms to rule;

when time servers are placed in high position
and unworthy men are charged to lead.

This is inflation to this generation –
to people who refuse to understand.

Dominant Powers

Listen to these words, you corporatists,
who combine, unify and destroy.

In your lust for growth and expansion
you have brought the world to chaos.

Your industrialisation of the lands
has caused the earth to be torn apart.

The pursuit of insatiable desire
has lowered the dignity of man.

You worthless men who promote your images,
creating confusion by your mindless schemes,

who hold to impersonal policies
and bring enterprise to an end:

as you assemble your statistics
you ostracise the people's goodwill;

you fill their time with paper and rules
and bind invention in chains.

Your companies will have no success
so long as you practise your foolish ways.

You have sacrificed the human dimension
to strive for control of the world.

Deus Ex Machina

Here is a word to those in command
who fail to command respect,

who run their staff like machines
and compress the human spirit.

You do not look behind intentions
or consider that men are frail;

you try to quantify their feelings
and objectify their inmost thoughts.

But as poor communication at home
divides family life,

so insecurity at work
causes a man to be anxious.

Anxiety leads to suspicion
and a suspecting man looks to himself;

he considers the needs of the moment,
he will not possess a generous soul.

Go to a lathe or a production line
and put your hands and minds to use!

Go into the quietness of a church
and think things through!

Noblesse Oblige

Now is the time to work together,
a time for divisions to be healed;

here is a moment of opportunity,
for co-operation rather than greed.

How great is your privilege of office
and the position in which you serve.

Consider your charge with care
and show others your concern.

Improve relations by honest means –
regard for all and freely given.

Treat your employees with respect –
remember they are human as you are.

Be honest with your workers
and you will have their loyal support.

Do not be quick to find fault,
but seek to praise and build.

Let each enjoy the fruits of labour
and the people use their talents aright.

Give due reward according to skill –
recognition, remuneration and rest.

To Captains of Industry

Is there an answer to inflation,
a solution to your economic ills?

Be selective in your commitments;
do what you have to do and do it well.

Reduce the spending of borrowed funds;
settle your bills when they are due.

Encourage the people to save,
and honour the prudent and wise.

Increase investment in business
by raising incentives to the ordinary man.

Control your industrial wastelands,
with their dereliction, pollution and blight.

Create new patterns of commerce
to meet the demands of the age.

Steer away from centralisation;
acknowledge those who do the work.

All people have a common duty
to develop their personal gifts.

Let competence be master of competition
and management be honourable, just and true.

— IX —

TO THE PROLETARIAT

The Perils of Social Ease

A nation is no longer great
when she fails to produce her goods.

A nation courts disaster
if she works according to rule.

A nation discloses her folly
when she spends all her money abroad.

A nation is finished
when she loses her self respect.

A nation without a soul
is destroyed by events in the world.

A nation that fails to pay her way
will have an ignominious end.

A nation that is afraid to work
will quickly waste away.

A nation that sits in comfort
will crumble like decaying bones.

A nation that seeks the easy life
will die in her sleep.

A nation that searches for utopia
will stand in her own grave.

To the Idle

This is to rude and lazy people
who are not prepared to work;

to those who only work to rule
and reduce the able mind to naught –

you idle people of the earth,
present in every walk of life,

who expect the world to support you
as you avoid the task in view.

What is our definition of a union?
A collection of greedy men.

What is our understanding of a company?
A gathering of the same.

You employed at the factory bench
who seek the latest dodge;

you business men in your dealings
who cheat to achieve success;

you with no employment
who fail to seek the chance:

you are ignorant of your responsibilities
but not of your payments and dues.

To Discontented Workers

Your country depends upon you:
you are the generators of wealth.

It is right that your voice should be heard
and that your case be put before the people.

It is not surprising that you are discontented
and prepared to withdraw your labour,

or that you should form your groups
to fight the threat of unemployment.

But be warned! You are being used by evil men
whose ideals would see the collapse of the land.

By all means push ahead with your claims
but consider the limits are drawn at disaster.

A mere tool of industrial policy
you are taken for granted by the nation;

as individuals loyal to your membership
you are pawns in a political game.

A mass of men herded together
you are open to insidious persuasion,

for fear is bred from ignorance
and militancy feeds on fear.

To Small Minded Unionists

You who have distorted the purpose of industry
and destroyed its potential for human good.

Selling your ideas to the bureaucrat
you conspire with reactionary schemes.

You prevent your nation moving forward
by wallowing in the issues of class;

you have held back technological progress
but condemn high unemployment in the land.

Creating false employment for the people
you have imagined immediate success;

you become their social benefactors
but take away their liberties.

Come now, we are tired of your cloth cap image,
we are bored by your plain affectation.

You have the power and the glory
but they will pass away.

Why cultivate ill temper at work?
Why waste away on pleasure and toil?

Why perpetuate a lower class image?
What a rich life is to be had by those who ask!

To Trade Unions

Trade unions, consider your foundation –
do not divide the people.

In your fight for principles and justice
remember the time honoured ways of God.

How can two draw up a contract
if one is of hollow deceit?

How can agreement be reached
under the threat of disruption and strife?

By reducing your demands
every man could be employed;

each one now receiving the dole
could be in work at a point of need.

Why should men be paid for doing nothing
when elsewhere there is no-one to work?

Why should you follow restrictive practices
when families are anxious for bread?

You who are responsible to industry,
who have held office over the years,

follow your philosophy to the limit –
share and share alike.

A Letter of Encouragement

Come now, you people in the west.
Establish a new hope in your hearts.

Gone are the days of craftsmanship
but in chaos they will return.

Gone are the days of the individual
but the collective will come to an end.

The genius of the west will be rediscovered
and founded upon the bedrock of hope.

Return to simpler ways,
to a time of craft and subtle skills.

Simplicity, brotherhood and freedom –
these are the tools for work.

Control the industrial machine
that dominates your lives;

man was not made by God
to be the victim of technology.

In the mines and in the factories,
in the heart of industry and at home,

in the pressures of competitive life,
let the qualities of God be known.

— X —

TO EGOTISTS,
FLATTERERS
AND SOCIALITES

Concerning Ambition

The man who is consumed by events
   is one who does not have peace,

for pride forbids tranquillity,
   self assertion brings unease.

Much anguish comes from pleasing the world,
   from trying to adjust to its covetous ways;

the anxious soul cannot be at peace
   nor will the troubled mind find rest.

How easy it is to buy one's friendship
   by placing oneself in the hands of fools;

how hard it is to gain affection
   by refusing to yield one's ideals.

A man may become a celebrity
   but not have a friend in sight;

he may win the admiration of many
   but be unable to love a single soul.

Look at the families of pretentious people –
   there lies the moral of the tale.

When a person outreaches his soul
   the balance of nature is disturbed.

To High Flyers

You who are anxious to get on,
to climb the ladder of material success.

Everywhere you seek promotion
but many remain frustrated.

Think for a moment of what is required
to reach the top of your trade.

Only a few reach the highest point
but how precarious the pas glissant.

Some of you cheat to attain it
and rob others of the chance to try,

seeking justification for yourselves,
willing to betray your neighbours.

Here is a word to you all,
and to those who seek to rule:

before you aspire to greatness
experience humility of heart.

Turn your lives in faith
and receive the grace of God.

Restore dignity and honour to your lives
and purpose will be bestowed upon your days.

A Thirst for Power

Why is the world as it is,
circling the whirlpool of chaos?

It is the desire for power,
the urge to become like God.

Greater councils, larger boroughs,
growing monopolies, villages, states,

churches, trade unions, people and homes –
all fall into the trap of power.

Let doctors who decide to be consultants
have the interests of their patients at heart.

Let clergy who desire to be bishops
seek to do the will of God.

Let politicians who crave key posts
prove their competence.

Let industrialists who covet high positions
achieve them through the fairest means.

Let councillors who promote their projects
cease to flatter themselves in public.

Let workers who claim higher pay
allow the rest of mankind to survive.

Integer Vitae Scelerisque Purus

This is advice to ambitious people
who depend upon public esteem.

Step by step is the way to success;
leaps and bounds are the way to ruin.

Do not look for instant acclaim:
there you will find no lasting peace.

Do not chase after false realities
nor try to become what you cannot be.

What is the finest way to human achievement?
To accept one's faults with a humble heart.

What is the surest path to well being?
The way of courage, endurance and hope.

Be independent of the opinions of others
and confirm your souls in the reality of God;

a quiet soul can discern the Spirit,
a tuned ear will hear his voice.

The one who proceeds in faith
will discover unlimited worlds;

he who holds fast to the truth
will triumph over evil.

The Challenge

How this world needs people with courage
who will say no to the pressures of life,

who are willing to reduce the tension
and become compassionate in their deeds,

who will make the first sacrifice
and refuse to betray their probity,

who will go only so far
and say that enough is enough,

who will conquer themselves
and control their lust for power!

Ah, says the innocent bystander,
the one who dare not become involved.

There is nothing I can do about this.
What difference would my actions make?

But as an evil man contributes to evil
so a good man helps the cause of good.

A little wickedness in an indifferent age
is the prescription for anarchy and ruin;

a little beauty in this fragmented life
may inspire you to glorious things.

— XI —

TO A
DECADENT SOCIETY

The Judgement

I speak to a world in the grip of greed,
pretending to be a caring world;

a world that would compromise its soul
for the sake of social ideals.

O you ignorant and defiled generation
whose morals are based on majority rule,

comforted by weak minded officials
who pander to your every need;

inert and undisciplined people
with no respect in your hearts,

getting away with as much as you can,
covetting your neighbour's goods:

consider your contribution to life –
what a miserable portion is your lot!

Who will rescue you from your empty lives
and restore character to your hollow deeds?

The paths of religion are too straight
for those who stumble like a drunken man.

The ways of morality are too hard
for people besotted by an easy life.

To Profligates

This is to people of the state,
to rich and poor alike;

to the governed and the governors,
to the powerful and the powerless.

Yield to temptation –
your pleasures will flee away.

Succumb to worldly pleasures –
they will consume you like fire.

Spend your money on luxuries –
complain at the end of the week.

Ask your employer for more –
he will raise the price of your goods.

Do your friend a favour –
charge him at top rates.

When your family asks for help –
how much are they prepared to pay?

Indulge yourselves in your squalor –
receive blessings from the state.

Be carried by the state –
it will carry you to the grave!

To Evil Thinkers

To those who make a fashion of immorality
and encourage the weak to indulge their desires,

who propound that sex is a free for all
and promote licentious living in the land;

who pedal drugs on street corners
and bring disease to humankind,

who scoff at old fashioned precepts
and treat religious belief with contempt.

Your liberation is simply a new word,
a cover for your crumbling integrity;

your equal rights merely a disguise
to pervert the human will.

You are unable to purify your lives
so why give reasons for your unclean ways?

You are incapable of restraining your desires
so why excuse the indulgence of your lusts?

Where are you now? What has been achieved?
What has happened to your cause?

You cannot convert my people, says the Lord.
You have chosen the way that will fail.

To the Slovenly

To those who make their own dirty conditions,
who are to blame and must reap the reward.

You wallow in your vulgar feculence
and bathe in the sewage of your thoughts.

You take no pride in your houses
and allow them to rot away.

You have made your own filthy surroundings
because you are full of sloth.

You spoil it for those who would try
because you have no self respect.

You would rather escape to the pub
than decorate your kitchen walls.

You would rather make merry in town
than nurture your children at home.

You would rather batter your offspring
than pull yourselves into shape.

Does man think that he is a body?
Then that shall be his dwelling place.

Does man behave as a machine?
Then that shall be his life.

To the Common Criminal

To those who commit crime
in order to survive.

Having lost all code of behaviour
you now resort to violence,

ready to strike with every weapon
in order to achieve your aim,

to steal what is not properly yours,
to possess things by dishonest means.

Cowards all! The thief is also a tough,
ready to break an old woman's skull.

But be warned, you men of deceit,
you will be brought to final justice.

You will be tried in the court of heaven.
God will judge in the end.

Do not assume that all is well with your days –
you stand before eternity or hell.

You who have been consumed
by vain devices and desires,

be conquered by the Spirit
of the transcendent God!

To the Fourth Estate

To those who work in television,
who deal in public opinion;

to those who write for the press
and stand for the liberty of speech.

Closing your ranks of self concern
you distort the truth for sensation;

searching everywhere for a loss of hope
you take your cameras to the depths of despair.

Your reporters gather like animals
at the downfall of public servants.

You exploit the violent nature of life
and create fashions of cultic desire.

But, you merchants of words,
your cause has been perverted;

you will soon be the tool of prejudice,
blinded from truth, forbidden to reveal it.

Which is the greater evil –
the denial of freedom or its abuse?

You have given in to the spirit of the age.
You have sold your souls for popular thought.

To the Masses

Here is a question for decadent people,
for the faceless masses of humankind –

people who have lost their religion
and are absorbed by material gain,

who are gripped in the vice of a system,
treated as numbers in a vast machine.

What is felt in the mortal mind?
How do you express your natural condition?

I am in this for all I can get;
my brother can go to the wall!

Are these your thoughts and intentions
or are you made of sterner stuff?

What great potential remains on earth
to increase your human happiness.

What a privilege it is to be alive –
but consider those who struggle to live.

Purify your existence;
remove the obstacles to love.

Demand less of life itself
and give more than you receive.

— XII —

TO DICTATORS,
TERRORISTS
AND FUNDAMENTALISTS

To Dictators

Militant and atheist dictators
who bring stress by the perversion of truth,

who collude with unworthy causes
to further your cruel desires.

How on earth can you be so proud
when your policies are such a disgrace?

How can you be such pompous fools,
pretending you are helping the poor?

You give false hope to the people
by distorting political aims;

you overturn the rule of order and law
by abusing the innocent and weak.

You are a threat to peace and justice
but God will ensure that you fail –

your works shall be judged
by man and his creator.

Do you think that human nature has changed?
Do you think that man is not the same as old?

You may seek to conquer the world
but will lose the integrity of your souls.

To Despots

Here is a word to those devious minds
who found their creed on envy and spite,

who have been enticed by a sense of power
and have absorbed false teachings of the age.

You are full of your own importance,
you must never be proved to be wrong;

you raise your voice when you are beaten
and bring threatening words to the weak.

You go about as if you owned the world,
inducing guilt by your haughty looks;

you lord it in a way not known before
and erect stone monuments to your name.

You are quite as bad as your adversaries,
focussing your minds on the evils of wealth,

following the history of corrupt institutions
in which power controls human life.

Do you know what a curse from God is?
Stand by – it is coming upon you!

His wrath will be felt in the nations,
his judgement in the collapse of your dreams.

To Terrorists

You terrorists who take no thought for others
and plant explosives in their midst.

Yes – you who have sunk into darkest evil
to kill your brothers for a cause.

What is your case worth?
Who will align with your aims?

Children torn apart by your invectives?
Women crippled by your weapons?

All for an ideal that has been lost –
buried with your first victim!

You may not believe in God
but he knows about you.

The final seconds of their temporal life
will become your eternal nightmare.

You desperate men of terror,
you are condemned by your deeds.

Your minds will hang suspended
in the black infinity of hell.

Repent and turn from your malignity.
Let God hear your case in peace.

To Cynics, Atheists and Sceptics

You think religion is out of date.
The modern mind has no room for God.

Well, here you have it, here it is.
Get ready for the truth in your waxed ears.

I have no time for you, says God,
neither you nor the apostasised church;

neither you nor your children
who cannot be bothered with the faith.

I have no favours set out before you.
If you persist in your mortal ways

you will be damned with inflation and ruin,
your greed will eat through your bones.

You will exist to see these words come true
and regret not having obeyed them.

You will perish before your time
and see your end before it is due.

You who say do not talk like this,
it disturbs our style of life –

I'll give you no comfort, says the Lord.
You will pay for your smug respectability.

To Militant Fundamentalists

You fanatics clothed in holy vesture
who perpetuate religious wars amongst mankind.

Corruption has entered your dealings.
Your souls have succumbed to ambition.

Before snow falls on the northern hills
your plans for disruption are made,

for winter brings cold to innocent people
but hardness of heart to the militant mind.

Blackmail, bribery and falsification –
these are the marks of your trade.

Your aim is to undermine the nations
and take the pickings for yourselves.

You spend your time on fatwahs and jehads
rather than improving your followers' lot.

You claim to champion the cause of God
but you are a totalitarian power.

I do not recognise your theses, says the Lord,
I do not see my Word in your schemes,

and those who do not stand for my Word
are against me in all their ways.

The Way Back

To all those engaged in conflict
and the struggle to survive.

A fractious man makes the heart race
but a man of peace will win respect.

Are you drawn into factions and strife?
You will not experience calm in your soul.

Are you torn by perfidious intrigue?
Then serenity will not be yours.

Does your pulse race with worldly pressure?
Better the heart responded to God,

for the true battle has been fought;
it has been won by Christ on the Cross.

And a word to those who doubt the way of love,
to those who are agnostic in their beliefs,

who hold no faith in their souls
nor trust in the laws of God:

peace is an honourable virtue,
a humble soul will reap its own reward.

Are these words made invalid
by those who do not believe in God?

— XIII —

TO THE
SUBJUGATED, TYRANNISED
AND OPPRESSED

Political Epigrams

When prejudice rules the nations
nothing will be achieved.

When leaders hold distorted beliefs
beware of the motive behind their talk.

When the voice of reason brings oppression
be sure the end is near.

When the principles of freedom are eroded
prepare for a time of chaos and despair.

When the ignorant decide your course of action
watch for a rift in order and peace.

When the incompetent rise quickly to power
stand by for the collapse of the land.

When the inarticulate speak on your behalf
listen to the sounds of the final act.

When the coarse and vulgar are established
the curtain begins to fall.

When the untutored shout for more and more
the end will come crashing down.

When wisdom departs from the people
dark tyranny begins.

A Satire

Here is a word to the collective,
to the people who think and speak alike –

herds that move about as one,
each man afraid to step out of line.

Amble forwards together, my people.
Do not look to the right nor to the left.

Do not look backwards over your shoulders,
neither look too far to the future.

How tame you are for your guardians,
for those who control you like sheep.

You imitate their thinking,
allured by their soothing tones.

Hush, my people! Do not cry!
Fold your arms and go to sleep!

Ssh, my people! Do not stir!
Let your little minds be still!

The state will turn your thoughts to dreams –
she shall comfort you as you rest.

Close your eyes to the night around you;
do not fret your minds – go to sleep.

A Warning of Traitors

There are enemies in your midst
who are out to wreck and destroy,

whose politics are based on prejudice,
their plans on outdated schemes.

Stand up to these evil doers
who attempt to negate what is good,

those who appeal to the baser self
and stir up strife in your souls;

the ones who assure you of your rights
but never mention duty,

who talk about demands
but seldom whisper trust.

They know you all respond gladly
to the orator who promises the earth,

for each one holds the self to heart
when it comes to meeting a need.

How evil prevails by consent of the people
as the power to resist is denied!

How democracy is pushed aside,
abused in the name of freedom!

Sleepers Wake!

Wake up, you tyrannised people!
  Shake yourselves from your sleep,

for the dawn has arrived in the evening,
  the hour of reckoning has come.

The day you dreamed would not happen
  is upon you – it is too late to run.

Now reveal your hopes for the future.
  Now let your thoughts be known to man.

According to the laws of history
  you are perched on the edge of ruin.

When chaos strikes who will help you then?
  Those who have urged you to help their cause?

They will flee from the cities to the hills;
  they will no longer be found among you.

You will be lost with the crowds,
  your wives and your children with you.

They who have your interests at heart,
  treacherous in their smooth talk,

they are taking you for a ride
  but they will not reveal your destination.

Towards Liberation

Confront those who urge confrontation,
who cannot confront themselves –

they are sowing the seeds of chaos;
you will reap the harvest of ruin.

The days of respectable silence are over.
Why be afraid to proclaim the truth?

Challenge oppressors with their wrong
and do not allow them to have their way.

These plumed and crested humbugs,
concerned only with their status,

who use weapons of material blackmail
to prop up their inhibiting weakness –

they despise the working classes
and ignore the helpless and poor;

they are intolerant of the blind and needy
and use all manner of means to suppress them.

Do they refuse to believe in eternity?
It shall be according to their faith.

It shall be measured to them with justice;
it shall be given to them with equal right.

To Citizens of the Earth

Ignore those who say there is no evil.
They are deceived in their desire to be safe.

What is evil but confusion, mistrust and ignorance?
Who can protect you in a benighted world?

It is by God that souls are saved
but wicked deeds stand condemned.

The state cannot replace the Creator
nor shall the world stand in his name.

Have nothing to do with infidels,
who rise and flourish in a material age;

you have been called in humility
and cannot survive by worldly power.

Pray for the ability to discern falsehood
and for courage to denounce it.

Ask of every dogma – is this of God?
every point of change – is this for the good?

Do not become one with arrogant men
who dismiss Christ as finished and dead.

They will die.
Christ will never die.

—— XIV ——

TO THE
ACADEMIC WORLD

To Universities – a Warning

How swiftly a fashion of thought
reduces the power of argument!

How easily an emotion of prejudice
stultifies the logic of thought!

How readily the academic mind gives way
to subtle perversions of truth!

How soon truth becomes a relative commodity
to be traded in university halls!

Reason is a personal currency,
bartered at a rate of exchange.

Concepts are controlled by politics,
and politics directed by trends.

Classics are derided and mocked,
greats are scourged and ignored.

Learning is scorned as elitism,
culture dismissed with contempt.

What is the criterion of meaning
and where shall reason be found?

Where is the seat of the intellect,
and how shall the truth be known?

To Pseudo Philosophers

A query for modern day thinkers
who have been bred on the fashion of doubt,

who perpetrate their thoughts to the masses
and hold that nothing is absolute.

Are not your ideas merely relative
to the condition of your times?

How dare you claim truth for your fashions?
In a decade they will be out of date.

My people have built their lives on your creeds –
now look at the results around you.

So much for you fraudulent thinkers
who say freedom, peace, and anything goes!

Does this disturb you, you hypocrites,
who lean against the glories of the past?

Does this upset you, you neologians,
who believe in a moral free for all?

Do these words cause irritation in your hearts
and resentment in your bones?

How you could be employed in greater things,
to discern a way forward for the people.

To Progressive Educationalists

Here is a word for you theorists,
reformers of wisdom, intellect and truth.

There is a difference between policy and practice
but you do not know what it means.

Because you are afraid of authority
your colleges are repositories of opinion.

Because you dismiss personal discipline
you fail to teach your children.

Because you do not believe in tradition
you propound laissez faire.

Because you put politics first
you are blind to intellectual needs.

Like a whirlpool spiralling downwards,
your theories have come to nothing:

your schools are battlegrounds of prejudice,
arenas for political correction.

Will such methods produce your leaders
or simply compel your children to conform?

And if they conform
to what do they conform?

To Dupes of Correction

A question for those who demonstrate
and shout in the streets for a cause.

How righteous is your life within?
How pure is the mouth that calls for justice?

When you return to your private lives
do you not ignore the moral law?

Are your ways so honest and pure
that you have no conscience of mind?

It is no use accusing your critics
or listing statistics to support you.

It is no use pointing to other factions.
You are the ones to hear these words.

You turn learning into politics
and make relatives absolutes.

You take politics beyond its brief,
dogmatists in your dealings with men.

Much better if you did an honest day's study
than add to the ranks of agitators.

How strong is your case when you stand alone,
empty of fashion, void of a crowd?

A Free Society

Liberty of movement, freedom of speech —
these are a citizen's rights.

The rights of man are universal
and cannot be limited by dogma or rule.

True freedom is not procured by force,
nor by the power of an aggressive mind;

it cannot be bought by prejudice
nor gained by irrational souls.

Freedom with no responsibility
is like a bottomless pit.

In the end it is spiritual freedom
which brings liberty to the human soul.

Grace, responsibility and hope —
these are the marks of a cultured age.

Erudition, trust and respect —
the cornerstones of a civilised race.

Free laws and a strong belief —
these are the foundations of society.

Joy and confidence in God —
that is the recipe for success.

— XV —

TO ARTISTS,
COMPOSERS
AND POETS

Epigrams of Taste

When a nation sustains no beautiful art
her vision has come to an end.

When fine arts vanish from your cities
be sure those cities will decay.

When artistic ideals collapse in confusion
prepare for a reaction from truth.

When the criterion of art is confused
then art is a label for anything.

When a writer is merely a function of society
he has parted with his soul.

When a poem consists only of material signs
the poet has missed his vocation.

When the composer writes for the critic
he has lost the spark of life.

When a nation does not foster genius
her ways become random and void.

When a nation forgoes creativity
life becomes sterile and cold.

When a land loses its soul
death looms on the horizon.

To Arts Councils

What are the priorities of national life?
Where do your civic responsibilities lie?

Who will suffer as a result of philistinism?
The innocent, religion and the arts.

Areas of life outside the production line,
elements of inventive pride and achievement,

unknown factors of national greatness –
all will fall in this spiritual drought.

The quality of your lives will decline,
the freedom of thought will decrease;

financial houses will decide your taste,
dull minds and ignorance will form the future.

Will you let this happen to your heritage?
Will you allow the fountain to dry?

What is the direction of your mind?
Indifference will lead to chaos.

To hold fast to creative choice
through the depths of mortality,

to believe in a way through
is strength for the soul.

Politics and Art

To civic authorities
and leaders of councils, a word.

People who live by imagination
are in touch with the springs of life.

A nation founded on heavenly vision
is a nation that will grow in strength;

her strength will be in depth and clarity
and her growth shall be in the Lord.

A country that lives according to purpose
is happier than one with no aim;

its citizens treat genius with respect
and treasure the history of original thought.

A worthy nation will proffer grants
to help the artistic mind;

she will become patron to ingenuity
and build galleries to new ideas.

Governments do not make works of art
but they can encourage them to flourish.

The arts and politics can work together
to raise the spirit of man.

To Sculptors and Composers

A word in the ear of the sculptor,
and composers of clever devices.

Your contraptions have caught you out,
their life extends to the moment of sale.

How shapeless are your tunes and images!
You have bored us with your clutter.

The junk you have created
is no longer fit for use.

O this stupid generation,
it has no aim!

O this indifferent cast of men,
modelled with impure clay!

Your vocation is to create dimensions
that reflect the harmony of spheres,

to find a coherence
between disjointed entities —

relations, patterns established,
grain and knot in the framework.

By variation and to order
let your syllables dance to music.

To Poetasters

A word to inferior poets,
inheritors of a fine tradition.

No rhyme nor reason in your verses.
Endless reams of subjective thoughts.

It does not matter what you say
as long as your name is in print.

It does not matter how you say it
as long as it is right for reviews.

How tragic that imitators of the word
should all be exactly alike.

Have you no talent, no original ideas?
Why do you feel the need to conform?

All poetry should be memorable;
a poem is reality itself.

Be concerned with that poetic
which permeates the existent,

reflecting the Name;
the mimesis of Word

extended to this lifetime
between the beginning and the end.

To Painters

Hear this word, you artists
who desecrate your gifts,

confounding the nature of form
with words to explain what you mean –

here a dab and there a line,
a blob and a splash and a shapeless hue –

each one doing his own thing,
producing a social design.

What is the true purpose of art
but to create, inspire and redeem,

to investigate space and time
and to search for a vision of heaven?

Art makes sense of the universe;
it is an account of the common forms of life.

The morphemic notation in art
is justified by one's experiences.

Generate colour and line for the future:
look to the Word for content and form.

Study the masters for yourselves:
there is the source of illumination.

To Genius

It is your right and duty to create –
do not forgo that right.

It is ordained that you should inspire –
do not lose your inspiration.

You are forerunners of a new age:
guard your privilege with care.

Know what you yourselves believe
and do not compromise your soul.

Do not waste your time on frivolities,
nor your energies on negative ways.

Do not allow your skills to be denuded,
nor let them be subject to political ends.

If you are destroyed by others
what good can you do in the world?

To see permanent significance in reality
is to perceive through an artistic eye.

True art is the flame of existence
residing in the soul of man;

it expresses man's life in the Spirit,
his relationship to God.

The Work of Art

A quest for the sublime in art
begins with the discernment of truth.

To stand in the truth at all times
is to be guided by spiritual light.

The artist considers the state of his soul
before his status in the world;

he will dedicate his genius to God
before engaging with his fellow men.

The artistic way finds a balance
between reason, feelings and the will;

the intellect, the heart and the senses
are transformed by a passion for life.

He who wishes to advance in art
must begin here in the world view.

The first step to discover reality
is to separate one's self from its image;

the mind can only determine the nature of things
when it becomes independent of everything.

Creativity begins with the I-Other relation;
it is independent of either and consists of both.

THE
DISCOURSE

Human Institutions

I tremble to set down these thoughts,
to publish them to a people I love.

Prayer must come before every action –
through prayer my confidence comes.

Trade unions cannot grant eternal life
nor politics purchase our redemption.

Economics cannot save a man from the grave
nor medicine prevent the pains of hell.

Education cannot provide a knowledge of God
nor social benefits bring the grace of Christ.

Culture cannot furnish men with the truth
nor philosophy bring lasting peace of mind.

Psychology cannot cure the fallen soul
nor sociology raise the dead to life.

The church cannot bind a broken world
nor theology calm a hungry soul.

Our institutions have no ultimate value
and their authority is not absolute.

How can we put our trust in them
or commit our lives to their cause?

To Alienated Man

Here is your tragedy, modern man:
you have become an alien in the world.

You will not accept things as they are –
the seasons and birth and death.

You interfere with the course of nature
and refuse to leave her alone.

The natural life you cannot endure
nor any longer live with yourself.

This is your tragedy, modern man:
you have set yourself against creation.

You systematise the contingent
and smooth over the pains of existence.

You destroy the earth for your resources
and despise the source of life.

You stand obdurately alone,
creating a future of doom,

for you cannot win the struggle –
nature will win in the end.

By your own ingenuity you will be removed;
the universe will cast you aside.

From a Secular Order

Is there a cure for the ills of the people?
Who will heal our wounds?

O for someone to perform the operation
to remove the disease from our lives,

to bind together a world of strangers
and point the way ahead for us all,

to rescue us from our afflictions
and act in the depths of our fallen state!

For we are ensnared in the trap of determinism
and the individual is helpless to act.

Evil is to do with things material,
the apparent shadow wherein is naught.

There our lives shall be
unless we change the object of our desire

and turn our flesh towards the Spirit
as we move in the emptiness of time.

Surely we are at an end,
unworthy to endure the pains of death?

Surely it would be better to be cast into nothing
than to experience a useless existence?

The Decline of Faith

You have lost your religion, O secular man.
The soul of nature has left your bones.

The sunset speaks no more to your heart,
the sound of birds is no longer heard.

The bare trees on a winter skyline,
the frozen ice of wayside ditches,

the purple heather rippling on the moors,
the bracken and fern in glen and dale –

they do not reach you, O secular man,
or fill your mind with praise and love.

Does the hawthorn, shaking in the breeze,
move your soul with gladness?

Do the stars in the heavens
haunt you with their distances?

Or the music of great composers
call to mind their inspiration?

Does the passing of time cause reflection,
or the span of years bring you nearer to God?

You forget your religion, O secular man,
and decay like the autumn leaves.

The Constitution

What, then, are the foundations of society?
Where are our roots to be found?

If we construct our lives in material terms
the structures pass away.

If we base our lives on physical things
they change with the passage of time.

Our senses reveal a contingent universe
in which nothing remains for the world of sense.

All that is perceived fades from our eyes,
our minds search in the darkest place.

Our future lies in the present,
the present is in the past.

What is here today will be gone tomorrow –
nothing is permanent in this changing void.

What are the principles of human behaviour?
Where can inspiration be heard?

What is the prescription for our broken state,
and how shall our life be restored?

Where can the light of existence be found
to continue through the spectrum of decay?

Divine Correction

Your religion has foundered on misbelief
and is no more a pilgrim's guide;

you have misunderstood the Faith
and distorted the shape of truth.

Do not employ the word 'God'
until you grasp its significance;

you use God in a tribal sense
and make him an object of fear.

Do not articulate 'sin'
until you know its meaning;

you sound the word in a moral sense
to condemn your fellow men.

Do not talk about 'religion'
until you know its implication;

you make religion a substitute
for the poetry of love.

Modern man, hear the voice of reality
in the tensions of your inner soul.

Listen to the words of Life
and publish them abroad.

THE
EPILOGUE

— I —

NEGATIONS

Vanity of Vanities

If you turn away from your destiny
and ignore the purpose of days,

if you direct the mind to finitude
and bind your soul to things,

if you fall into an endless circle
and pursue the interests of self,

then indeed you are acquainted with sin
and experience your own futility.

If you focus your heart on the present
and dissemble the future and past,

if you descend to the zero of being
and cast your lot into nothing,

if you experience the death of existence
before the opening of your grave,

then indeed you are acquainted with sin
and experience your own futility.

Mankind sinks to the lowest depths
or climbs to the greatest heights,

but the noblest thing of all
is when man overcomes his faults.

The Seven Deadly Sins

Pride centres the universe on ego
and brings the soul to nothing.

Avarice is a love of opulence
extending to the material plane.

Lust is a concern for the flesh
to the neglect of the spiritual life.

Envy is pride of possession
and desire for the wealth of others.

Gluttony is concentration upon particulars
to the disdain of the whole of man.

Anger is the binding of the human heart
to prejudice, fear and hate.

Sloth ignores the Other
and considers only the I.

On Guilt

Guilt corrodes the human frame
and takes strength from the soul.

Guilt arises out of judgement
and accompanies a sorrowing heart.

Guilt destroys innocent joy
and brings heaviness of mind.

Guilt robs man of his liberty
and chains him to the past.

Guilt turns the spirit sour
and causes suspicion to rule.

Guilt reveals a broken relationship
and cuts man off from his roots.

On Fear

Fear is the portent of failure,
the admission of a loss of hope.

Fear is the negation of what is possible,
the denial of aspiration and faith.

Fear is to the future
as guilt is to the past.

Fear stultifies the spirit
and paralyses the human will.

Fear asserts the inferiority of selfhood
in the lack of resolution and hope.

Fear determines human destiny
in the absence of spiritual power.

Social Litanies

For continuing our obsession with sin
while ignoring the truth of the Word:
O Lord forgive.

For our inability to create respect
except in the structures of power:
O Lord forgive.

For always keeping others at a distance
by holding jealously guarded secrets:
O Lord forgive.

For our imported schemes and practices
which take no account of humankind:
O Lord forgive.

For the exploitation of our fellow men
and the plunder of the world's resources:
O Lord forgive.

For using people to calculated ends
which destroys their personal freedom:
O Lord forgive.

For assuming a right to everything
and desiring all for ourselves:
O Lord forgive.

Political Litanies

For perpetuating the secular myth
that man is merely a machine:
> *O Lord forgive.*

For putting our trust in technology
and thereby losing our faith:
> *O Lord forgive.*

For succumbing to the power of the state
and yielding our souls to the world:
> *O Lord forgive.*

For legislating our confusion
and turning our chaos into laws:
> *O Lord forgive.*

For the humbug of pretending to love
when love is a mere expedient:
> *O Lord forgive.*

For abusing the lovely in the world
and failing to lead a simple life:
> *O Lord forgive.*

For losing sight of the eternal
and putting ourselves in your place:
> *O Lord forgive.*

— II —

RELIGIOUS
VIRTUES

The New Way

Consider the world around you –
for every evil there is greater good.

Evil is on the losing side;
good will triumph in the end.

Pray for release from vanity
and renew the spirit of your being;

the whole universe will rejoice
with one who conquers his ways.

Recognise your limitations:
they will vanish from your sight;

from the moment of restoration
the potential of time is declared.

Do not mingle with the crowd
to confirm your dependence of mind;

do not reach beyond your grasp
but improve what is within your power.

Respect the laws of creation –
they will save you from losing your soul.

Trust in the ways of righteousness –
they will not desert you in the moment of need.

On Grace

Grace is located in the given;
  it is the source of strength for man.

Grace brings hope to the downhearted
  and builds up the fallen and dismayed.

Grace stands upright and secure
  through circumstance and trial.

Grace is the assurance of achievement,
  the promise of greatness in life.

Grace meets human existence
  at the nth root of destiny.

On Redemption

Redemption is the pattern of reality,
an image of the structure of life.

Redemption transforms the concepts of mind
and renews the perspective of being.

Redemption is a cure of the soul;
it revives the strength of will.

Redemption leads to a conversion of heart
and rejuvenates the understanding.

Redemption is the quintessence of religion,
the lifeblood of human endeavour.

On Repentance

Repentance is to turn the mind
away from the centre of self.

Repentance is to alter direction
and aim towards infinite life.

Repentance regenerates hope
and invigorates the intellect.

Repentance reforms the future
by declaring freedom from the past.

Repentance is a necessary condition
to receive forgiveness in the soul.

On Forgiveness

Forgiveness accompanies repentance
and restores the state of man.

Forgiveness follows a change of heart;
it is not attendant upon regret.

Forgiveness means eradication
of all that binds l'élan vital.

Forgiveness is release of the soul
from the bondage of sin and death.

Forgiveness is an association of conscience
that turns present loss into future gain.

On Hope

Hope is affirmation of the soul
in a world of increasing materialism.

Hope is the interfacing link
between the individual and the universe.

Hope is the incursion of eternity
into the dimension of time.

Hope is the potential of momentum
in the nucleus of present events.

Hope is the eternal means
by which energy is converted to power.

On Prayer

Prayer binds one person to another
in the freedom of spiritual truth.

Prayer reaches towards infinity
and brings man into the presence of God.

Prayer is the trajectory of faith,
the path to the realisation of being.

Prayer is the controlling of circumstance
according to the will of God.

Prayer is a cosmic potency
that transcends the continuum.

— III —

FRUIT
OF THE SPIRIT

The Criterion

As the trained mind distinguishes truth from falsehood,
so the enlightened soul can tell right from wrong.

As there are mathematical laws in the universe,
so there are rules of the moral world.

As logic is to thought,
so religion is to existence.

As objects in space obey physical precepts,
so the righteous adhere to ethical law.

God has ordered the natural world,
and formed the axioms of holiness.

He ordains a code of experience
to discern the poetry of being.

Acts of faith express an intention to live
according to certain spiritual laws.

The Ten Commandments are more than rules:
they point to the principles of life.

This is a generation who have gone astray;
they have wandered from the ways before them,

but they can return and save their sorrow,
begin again and not be cut down, says the Lord.

On Love

Love is the deepest relation of all
between fellow human beings.

Love is sympathy from the heart;
it is the pain of the thorn of the rose.

Love is the readiness to stay
when others rise to move away.

Love is the song of the universe,
the music of the creative act.

On Joy

Joy brings cheer to social concerns
and rids the heart of woe.

Joy brings completion to man;
it is the fulfilment of hope.

Joy is a cheerful soul,
full of assurance and love.

Joy is colour, romance and bliss;
it is the morning of eternal spring.

On Peace

Peace is the present moment
sanctified by the presence of God.

Peace is a point in time
extending towards infinity.

Peace is not I against Other;
it is found in unity and love.

Peace is the harmony of heaven,
the stillness of the mathematical curve.

On Patience

Patience is found in the sacrament of being
and is sustained in the practice of hope.

Patience is not the absence of will
but absorption of self within the whole.

Patience never gives up
nor accepts that all is lost.

Patience is the assurance of spirit
in a contingent world.

On Kindness

Kindness is care for another
without cost of return.

Kindness is concern for the downtrodden
when others pass them by.

Kindness is selfless consideration
by one human being for another.

Kindness is a reflection of love,
the natural feeling of the Christian heart.

On Goodness

Goodness is the recognition of worth
bestowed upon human beings by God.

Goodness is expressed in innocent joy;
it is not laboured or controlled.

Goodness is no intellectual construction;
it springs from the heart.

Goodness begins as an attitude of mind;
it is founded in the spirit of man.

On Faith

Faith is a vision of what is possible,
the power by which things are done.

Faith is a vital human spirit
that sweeps away mistrust.

Faith is the spur to action
that dismisses hesitation and doubt.

Faith controls human destiny
and leads man to freedom and peace.

On Meekness

Meekness is the tenderness of Christ's spirit
that leads another towards the love of God.

Meekness does not patronise or condescend;
it treats others with respect and trust.

Meekness allows a person to be;
it does not stultify or condemn.

Meekness is an attraction to man;
it puts an end to fear and dread.

On Temperance

Temperance is strength in every weakness;
it stirs the human will.

Temperance does not derive from circumstance;
it is dependent upon grace of life.

Temperance takes a useless situation
and invests it with the power of God.

Temperance is self control
in the context of affluence.

A Hymn of the Spirit

Let the state control your lives –
the Spirit brings freedom to man.

Let the bureaucracy increase –
the Spirit is boundless and free.

Let the earth be nationalised –
the Spirit is your heavenly home.

Let the state order all things –
the Spirit will triumph in the end.

Let the state create laws and courts –
the Spirit judges the heart of man.

Let the world be sorrowful in its folly –
the Spirit brings revival of heart.

Let the world laugh and sing –
the Spirit brings true joy to man.

Let the state seek to possess your soul –
the Spirit will bring release.

The Holy Spirit of God
is life and health and truth –

PRAISE TO THE SPIRIT.

— IV —

POLITICAL
VIRTUES

A Prayer for Peace

O Creator of all that exists,
who alone can restore the world to faith,

I dream of an age of peace
when the years of war roll away,

when dark horizons cease
and the sun lights up the day,

when the night becomes a time for faith
and the day fulfills our hope.

O the tension that makes us scream,
the pressure that tears our lives apart,

the dilemmas between self and others,
the conflict of interests in the world.

Lord, convert our gloom to gladness,
our weapons to tools of peace.

Grant vision to this disordered age;
confront us with the road ahead.

Lead us towards integrity;
restore harmony to our deeds.

We will thank you with grateful hearts
and glorify your name.

Liberty of the People

Liberty is an extension of spiritual space
by regeneration of the human will.

Liberty is a right of male and female,
for both are equal in the sight of God.

Liberty denied to others
betrays the dignity of man.

Liberty abused in oneself
imprisons all humanity.

A nation that treasures her liberty
must be vigilant to retain it,

but true liberty is found in the soul
and is preserved in a person's heart.

On Freedom

Freedom is the right to think;
it is the privilege to be.

Freedom is space through which to move,
the time in which to act.

Freedom is bestowed upon individuals
when they allow each other to be free.

Freedom cannot be bought or sold;
it is given or betrayed by the will.

Freedom from oppression
is the desire of enlightened man.

Freedom from rules and regulations
is the goal of the mystical quest.

On Justice

Justice is the interpretation of God's law;
it springs from the desire to be free.

Justice thrives on liberty and truth;
it is denied by repression and falsehood.

Justice is a measure of balance
between the rights of one and all.

Justice is the distribution of rights
throughout the whole community.

Justice is the relationship of freedom
between an individual and society.

Justice derives from the creator;
it is the implementation of truth.

On Truth

Truth is not afraid of lies,
neither does it fear distrust.

Truth is not enhanced by repression,
neither is it upheld by force.

Truth is served by justice
and is born out of freedom.

Truth will survive oppression
and stand in the midst of wrong.

Truth is not a social expedient,
nor handmaid to political gain.

Truth stands alone,
unchanged by the fashions of time.

On Compassion

Compassion is understanding in truth;
it is to suffer on behalf of others.

Compassion is not an excuse
to explain away moral fault and sin.

Compassion is discipline and strength;
it is exercised in self control.

Compassion is not companion to evil intent,
nor the inversion of the laws of God.

Compassion does not rush to agree;
it weighs action with the wisdom of Christ.

Compassion is unconditional acceptance
in the grace and spirit of Christ.

Thanksgivings

Thank God for those who are prepared to speak
when the foolish crowd watches in silence.

Thank God for those who seek to preserve
what corrupt society plans to destroy.

Thank God for those who are prepared to work
surrounded by complacent people.

Thank God for those with social conscience
who show concern for the poor and weak.

Thank God for the pure and simple hearted
who survive the flood of fools.

Thank God for those who save others
when evil forces seek to kill.

Thank God for those who simply love
without the need for a political creed.

Thank God for those who strive for justice
in the face of social oppression.

Thank God for those who simply care
without dogma to rule their hearts.

Thank God for the ones who find God
in quietness and resolute endurance.

— V —

ARTICLES
OF FAITH

The Mystery of Life

Consider, man, the universe around you,
how the stars shine in the darkness.

You can never reach the end of time
or explore the outer regions of space.

Here you receive your existence
and pursue your everyday toil;

surrounded by increasing mystery
you begin and come to an end.

Why therefore do you lack humility?
Why be so anxious to prove your worth,

to appoint yourselves to positions of esteem
or puff your souls before the world?

Be gracious in your lives,
choose the right way!

Shine through the darkness of this age
with humility, charity and acts of peace.

Do not be discouraged by those who fall
or by your failures and shortcomings.

If you aim in the right direction
you will recover and never fail.

On Heaven

Heaven is not wholly other than time and space;
it is part of the continuum.

Heaven is not identified with space and time;
the two are contradefined.

Heaven does not come after life
following the point of death.

Heaven is the quality of life
which transcends the world of sense.

Heaven is at the heart of reality,
existing throughout the universe and beyond.

Heaven is the context of each time instant,
and touches time at the point of meaning.

Heaven is a moment in time lived for ever,
each act of love and joy made permanent.

Heaven is the fullness of grace remembered
as the significance of time deepens to eternity.

On Hell

Hell is the vacuum of reality,
a loss of the structure of being.

Hell is a domain of falsity
in society and individual man.

Hell is the negation of God
in the perpetual cycle of sin.

Hell is the nullity of soul,
the displacement of the freedom to be.

Hell is the infinite duration of time
in a meaningless existence.

Hell is a permanent state of nonbeing,
the dwelling place of shadows.

Hell is the absence of fact,
the ghostland of unreality.

Hell is the opposite of heaven,
the converse of eternal life.

On True Religion

Religion is the prosody of being
between persons, terms and things.

Religion describes the universe;
it also constitutes reality.

Religion shows purpose behind contingency
and reveals the councils of heaven.

Religion is known in relationships
and is reflected in the reverence for life.

Religion is the fountain of liberty;
its law is the law of love.

Religion and God's love do not contend;
love expresses the deeper law.

Religion explores the mystery of creation
in the programme of evolutionary law.

One cannot question the laws of existence;
the laws of existence precede thought.

On The Holy Spirit

The Holy Spirit is the root of a righteous nation,
the foundation of a permanent people.

The Holy Spirit is mediated through the universe
in the relations between I and Other.

The Holy Spirit is the essence of man,
the spiritual depths of his existence.

The Holy Spirit is both sorrow and joy
in this mysterious tract of time.

The Holy Spirit is the power of life;
it is the force behind human destiny.

The Holy Spirit is the constant of integration
between the first term and infinity.

The Holy Spirit is found in symmetry,
in proportion, order and form.

The Holy Spirit is God's act of conception
dwelling in the spirit of man.

On Christ

Christ is one with God the Father
and one with man on earth.

Christ is human and divine,
perfect body and perfect soul.

Christ is the meaning of science and art,
the fulfilment of the purpose of God.

Christ is life and truth,
the logic of the creative act.

Christ is the Word of the universe;
he recreates the human spirit.

Christ is the Word incarnate,
whose power gives life to all.

Christ is the total man,
the definition of his being.

Christ is the Lord of all,
beyond whom all religions fade away.

Of God and Eternity

God is the foundation of being;
  he is the origin of life.

God is the Eternal Other
  without magnitude or shape.

God is infinity and finitude;
  he dwells everywhere and forever.

God is life in its everlasting form,
  existing throughout eternity.

God is the founder of the heavens,
  the inceptor of all creation.

God binds all things together
  and inheres between particulars.

God abides in the midst of change
  between eternity and the universe.

God stands at the core of existence
  and reigns in the highest heaven.

The Origin of Time and Space

God is first cause of the universe
and prime mover of the stars.

God is inventor of the atom,
the energy behind all things.

God is the originator of time,
the architect and builder of space.

God is author of the singularity;
he is the axis of space-time correlates.

God is the beginning of actuality;
he is the end of all matter.

God alone rules the ages
and controls the particles of being.

God is order and structure
at the interface of time and space.

God is the unity of creation,
the harmony of the universe.

The Domain of Space-Time Events

God exists in the outer universe
  beyond the silences of time.

God exists in the smallest particle,
  within the minutest element of being.

God acts in the galaxies of space,
  and in the formula $((Gh/c^3)^{1/2} = 10^{-33}$ cms.)

God is potentially present
  in the black holes of space.

God exists in the process of time
  and in the co-ordinates of existence.

God is the determinant
  behind each locus in quo.

God exists in events
  as events cohere in God.

God is the truth of science,
  the criterion of art.

The Soul of the Universe

God is life and light.
Existence is his name.

God is peace and stillness;
he is wisdom and strength.

God is the foundation of love,
the composer of laws.

God is personal spirit
who communes with man.

God stands behind the mind of man;
in him there is logic and truth.

God exists in creativity;
his love extends to the heart of man.

God is the destiny of mankind,
the eternal purpose behind creation.

In the beginning and the end –
GOD.

Psalm

You are quietness and peace,
Soul of the Universe.

You are the mystery of creation,
the unknown Spirit of life.

You are hidden in the intricacies of matter,
beyond the edge of time.

You are silence and strength,
Soul of the Universe.

You exist forever, boundless and free;
you are infinite and without frame.

Eternal Spirit of the deeps,
why do we give you a name?

You are life and existence,
Soul of the Universe.

You are the wind that moves the trees;
you are the energy of the sun.

You are the power of the mighty seas,
the endless search of man.

— VI —

TO MANKIND –
A
MESSAGE OF HOPE

To the Present Age

Here is a word for this generation,
  born into conflict and strife.

Before the ending of the age,
  before the turning of the years,

you shall stand alone
  at the beginning of a new age.

Be full of courage,
  be of strong hope.

Turn your eyes to the Cross –
  be renewed in the might of God.

You who are dispirited
  and find your lives a burden:

remember the empty tomb,
  the dawn of eternal light,

zero – infinity becoming,
  desolate but full of victory.

Trust in God,
  do not despair.

There is lasting purpose for the human race.
  That purpose shall be fulfilled.

Christieth the Saviour

God's humility stands supreme –
for Christ died alone on the Cross.

The Cross is a symbol of hope,
eternal triumph in a finite world.

Christ took his redeeming power
to the stillness of the grave,

to the zones of death and hell
between nothingness and eternity.

He gave his soul to death;
he filled life's zero with his being.

Therefore, God has conquered death
and sin is broken by eternal grace.

No sin is beyond Christ's redemption;
no man stands outside his love.

Is a man confused in this life?
Let him find order in Christ.

Is he consumed by the ways of the world?
Let him turn to the Scriptures for the Word.

Is he bowed low by his shortcomings?
Let him find his wellbeing in the Lord.

The Christic of Grace

The Word of God is not devoid of purpose,
though the world may despise his name;

his knowledge of the world is complete,
his teaching sufficient for your needs.

Do not allow the Word to become a byword
nor cause the dignity of God to fall;

you are the beloved of the risen Christ,
your nobility is found in his blood.

Do not apologise for the Word –
he was there in the beginning of time;

hold fast to the truths of the Gospel;
have courage to start again.

Do you dread dealings with your fellow men?
Be of Christ.

Do you fear the ways of the world?
Be of Christ.

Do you lack faith in all you do?
Be of Christ.

If you stand in the fellowship of Christ
you will experience his power in life.

Christat the Mediator

In Christ there is no jealousy or contention,
    no suspicion or mistrust;

in him there is perfect freedom
    and grace untouched by human law.

In Christ there is no fear of man,
    neither is there subservience or doubt;

he renews the spirit of man
    and raises him when he is low.

In Christ there are no dogmas of kind;
    divisions find no place in him,

neither Roman nor Protestant,
    nor Orthodox nor Free.

In Christ perfect harmony dwells;
    no factions are found in the Son of God,

neither politics of right wing nor of the left,
    neither communist nor capitalist ways.

In Christ there is perfect reconciliation
    of man to God and man to man.

There is no disunity in Christ,
    neither is disharmony found in him.

The God of Hope

When all seems lost and void
put your trust in Jesus Christ.

How can you despair if you know the Lord?
Put your whole confidence in him.

In the darkness of your mortal souls
he will shine with brilliant light;

in the gloom of your daily lives
he will reveal his unsearchable gifts.

Commit your lives to your Saviour,
offer them in the quietness of prayer;

he will transform them into new creations
and lift the burden of their toil.

How the infinite Spirit can be explored
by one who follows the steps of faith.

Let faith be the effect of your being
and you will live in a state of grace.

Christ is your hope for the future;
he is the way, the truth, the light.

He is the archetype of all that is to come,
the consummation of the eternal hope of man.

— VII —

TO THE
THIRD MILLENIUM

Hope for a New Age

Come now, turn from your ways, my people.
 I will restore grace to your lives once more.

I will give confidence to your leaders
 and trust in the work I set before you.

I will remove your negative thoughts
 and rid you of your recurring ills.

The world will look to you with hope
 and see honour in your dealings with men.

The nations will look to you with joy;
 you will grow in strength and abound with faith.

You will shine as a light from the mountains –
 a searchlight beaming from the highest hills.

You will regain your love for the people
 and a greatness of worship within your walls.

Integrity I will grant to your institutions;
 you will survive the fire that burns in the world.

Come! Accept the challenge I have measured to you!
 Strengthen your hearts for the fight ahead!

You stand at the threshold of mystery,
 at the dawn of a spiritual age.

God's Call

Let the nations shout and clamour!
Let them go ahead with their plans!

You have your calling and salvation –
the path is laid for you.

If the nations go down
must you follow?

If empires collapse
do you give in?

Though you have deserted me in this age
I have not cut you from my thoughts.

Though you have strayed from my ways
I have not departed from you.

Though you have built cities like idols
and worship the creations of your hands,

for all this my Spirit remains with you
and your people are still in my heart.

Hear the voice of the Lord your God:
you are only at the beginning of time.

My thoughts are of the future,
before the ending of the age.

A Glimpse into the Future

What are the glories of this age?
What are the virtues of your time?

Are you a people entirely without hope?
Are you chained forever to the past?

What can be achieved in this mortal life?
Where is the first light for this generation?

The time is coming when your children will smile
and hope shall be nourished in the world.

Their hearts will no longer be heavy with fear,
their minds will be clear like a mountain stream.

Their souls will be freed from selfish concern,
their eyes will shine with perfect light.

Peace will sweep through the industrial lands;
furnaces and foundries will be fired with hope.

Prosperity will come to harbours and shoreways
and commerce will flourish in her honest ways.

To the lonely will come a fullness of joy,
to the downhearted an upsurge of strength.

Nations will flock to the churches,
and the people abide in the kingdom of God.

Harmony in Creation

Eagles will guard the highlands
   and deer will walk on the moors,

salmon will return to the rivers
   and geese to the outer isles;

elm trees will return to the cities
   and willows will flourish in towns,

shore lines will be free from pollution
   and valleys and hills will stand

when man once more accepts the Lord
   and walks in the ways of heaven.

Return to God, my people,
   establish yourselves in hope.

In the hillsides and on the moors
   let the winds reveal the glory of God;

may his Spirit be felt in the teeth of the gale
   and be known in the raindrops of spring.

Come, search for hope in deep drifts of snow,
   where hedgerows are hidden from fields;

find it in the inner reaches of your minds,
   in the communion between God and your souls.

A New Dawn

What will be the nature of the third millenium?
How will the story be told?

What will the new age bring?
What hope for the world?

A new order will be established in the earth,
a frame of thought by which to live;

a disciplined life free from self,
a pure way of living in the land;

a life directed by the enlightened soul,
inspired by thought and care;

a sharing of power amongst the people
with deep commitment to hope;

an intellectual, moral and spiritual harmony
focussed upon beauty, grace and truth;

a renaissance for art and science,
a philosophy for all mankind.

There will be no division in God's Millenium,
no force or compulsion from above;

there will be joy amongst the people
when the day of triumph dawns.

The Vision of Heaven

A mighty vision will come to the people,
    one in which men shall be glad,

in which the flesh will yield to the Spirit
    and material needs give way to the soul –

a sweeping clean of the older forms
    and a return to eternal truths;

a world in which all men are equal,
    where privilege is counted as life itself;

where humanity triumphs over evil
    and peace reigns throughout the world;

where mankind discovers the laws of God
    in the mysteries of science;

where man can fulfill his purpose
    in the mystical quest of art;

where doubt is removed from the mind of man
    and faith stands assured of the Lord.

The new man will break the shackles of time
    and burst open the boundaries of space.

The whole universe will shout in praise
    and the galaxies resound to the glory of God.

INDEX

Index of Titles

INDEX

Index of First Lines

INDEX

INDEX

INDEX